@Copyright 2020 by Christine Aguilar - **All rights**.

This document is geared towards providing exact and reliable information in regards to the topic and issue covered. The publication is sold with the idea that the publisher is not required to render accounting, officially permitted, or otherwise, qualified services. If advice is necessary, legal or professional, a practiced individual in the profession should be ordered.

Under no circumstance will any legal responsibility or blame be held against the publisher for any reparation, damages, or monetary loss due to the information herein, either directly or indirectly.

Legal Notice: The book is copyright protected. This is only for personal use. You cannot amend, distribute, sell, use, quote or paraphrase any part or the content within this book without the consent of the author.

Disclaimer Notice: Please note the information contained within this document is for educational and entertainment purposes only. Every attempt has been made to provide accurate, up to date and reliable complete information. No warranties of any kind are expressed or implied. Readers acknowledge that the author is not engaging in the rendering of legal, financial, medical or professional advice. The content of this book has been derived from various sources. Please consult a licensed professional before attempting any techniques outlined in this book.

CONTENTS

Introduction 5

The Benefits of Owning Your Own Cuisinart Ice Cream Maker 6

How to Use the Cuisinart Ice Cream Maker? 7

Recipe Tips 8

Simple Ice Cream Recipes 9

    Vanilla Ice Cream 9

    Butter Pecan Ice Cream 10

    Chocolate Ice Cream 11

    Fresh Strawberry Ice Cream 12

    Mocha Ice Cream 13

    Key Lime Ice Cream 14

    Vegan Ice Cream 15

    Peach Ice Cream 16

    Mocha Madness Ice Cream 17

    Apricot Ice Cream 18

    Rhubarb Swirl Ice Cream 19

    Blackberry Ice Cream 20

    Orange Creamsicle Ice Cream 21

    Pineapple Ice Cream 22

    Purple Taro Ice Cream 23

    Eggless Pistachio Ice Cream 24

    Coconut Ice Cream 25

    Cinnamon Ice Cream 26

    Coffee Toffee Ice Cream 27

    Banana Pudding Ice Cream 28

Custard Style Ice Cream Recipes 29

    Vanilla Frozen Custard 29

    Basic Custard Ice Cream with Sea Salt 30

    Custard Chocolate Ice Cream 31

    Custard Cantaloupe Ice Cream ... 32

    Turmeric Ice Cream 33

    Mango Ice Cream 34

    Rocky Road Frozen Custard Ice Cream 35

    Honey Ice Cream 36

    Pumpkin Custard Ice Cream 37

    Custard Cream Gelato 38

    Thermomix Licorice Ice Cream .. 39

    Barbados Custard Ice Cream 40

    Strawberry Matcha Custard Ice Cream 41

    Banana Custard Ice Cream 42

    Cookies and Cream Ice Cream .. 43

    Pralines and Cream Custard Ice Cream 44

Double Espresso Ice Cream 45

Nutella Ice Cream 46

Malted Milk Chocolate Ice Cream.... 47

Dark Chocolate Cheery Custard Ice Cream 48

Frozen Yogurt Recipes 49

Healthy Greek Frozen Yogurt 49

Strawberry Vanilla Frozen Yogurt .. 50

Frozen Cantaloupe Yogurt 51

Blueberry Frozen Yogurt 52

Chocolate Frozen Yogurt 53

Peach Frozen Yogurt 54

Tart Frozen Yogurt 55

Strawberry Basil Frozen Yogurt...... 56

Neapolitan Frozen Yogurt................ 57

Dulce De Leche Frozen Yogurt 58

Berry Berry Frozen Yogurt.............. 59

Blackberry Sugar-Free Keto Frozen Yogurt.. 60

Lemon Frozen Yogurt 61

Lemon Blueberry Frozen Yogurt 62

Maple Frozen Yogurt........................ 63

Matcha Frozen Yogurt...................... 64

Peach Mango Frozen Yogurt............ 65

Feta Frozen Yogurt........................... 66

Mint Greek Frozen Yogurt............... 67

Dark Chocolate Coconut Frozen Yogurt 68

Buttermilk Frozen Yogurt 69

Pumpkin Frozen Yogurt 70

Watermelon Strawberry Frozen Yogurt 71

Pistachio Berry Frozen Yogurt 72

Mulberry Frozen Yogurt.................. 73

Sorbets 74

Mango Tango Sorbet........................ 74

Meyer Lemon Sorbet 75

Orange Sorbet 76

Lemon Strawberry Sorbet............... 77

Watermelon Sorbet.......................... 78

Easy Coconut Sorbet........................ 79

Mango Pineapple Sorbet 80

Lime Sorbet 81

Strawberry, Nectarine, Orange, Banana Sorbet.................................. 82

Kiwi Sorbet....................................... 83

Pineapple Sorbet.............................. 84

Avocado Sorbet 85

Peach Sorbet..................................... 86

Lime-Mango Sorbet 87

Summer Sorbet 88

Berries Sorbet 89

Passion Fruit Sorbet 90

Grape Sorbet 91

Cherry Mango Sorbet 92

Mulberry Ginger Sorbet 93

Frozen Ice Cream Desserts 94

Frozen Banana Split 94

Turtle Brownie Ice Cream 95

Oreo Ice Cream Cake 96

Strawberry Ice Cream Milk Shake ... 97

Vanilla Ice Cream Sponge Cake 98

Vanilla Peanut Butter Layer 99

Oreo Ice Cream Bar Dessert 100

Caramel Frozen Squares 101

Frozen Pistachio Ice Cream Dessert 102

Ice Cream Sliders 103

Sugar Cookie Sandwich with Ice Cream 104

Ice Cream Pizza 105

Berry Ice Cream Cake 106

Rhubarb Ice Cream Cake 107

Frozen Nanaimo Pie 108

Introduction

Making your own desserts need not be difficult. In fact, it is the most fun and fulfilling thing to do. And now that summer is here, the best desserts that you can make are cold ones – ice cream! This book is dedicated to teaching you how to make your favorite frozen treats right at the comforts of your home. But contrary to many misconceptions, making ice cream is never difficult as long as you have an ice cream maker. And what better way to make your ice cream than to have your own Cuisinart Ice Cream Maker

The Benefits of Owning Your Own Cuisinart Ice Cream Maker

What makes the Cuisinart Ice Cream Maker special is that it is designed to make ice cream making an easy task. In fact, it is very convenient and economical to make your own frozen desserts at home. Not only do you know what kinds of ingredients go into your ice cream, but you also have saved money as you can make frozen desserts with ingredients that you currently have at home. While these are the benefits of any ice cream maker, the Cuisinart Ice Cream maker offers so much more. Below are the benefits of owning your own Cuisinart Ice Cream Maker.

- **Adding ingredients is a breeze:** This kitchen appliance comes with an ingredient spout that allows you to add ingredients in a breeze. You can add nuts, chips, and other ingredients without interrupting the freezing cycle. This means that the internal temperature of the ice cream chamber is kept constant thus the consistency of the ice cream is better compared to conventional ice cream makers.
- **Transparent Lid:** The lid of the Cuisinart Ice Cream Maker is transparent so you can check the entire freezing process as well as the progress of your dessert. For security purposes, the lid easily locks to the base, so it does not come off easily during the churning process.
- **Comes with a powerful mixing arm:** Mixing troubles are all in the past thanks to the powerful mixing arm of the Cuisinart Ice Cream Maker. The mixing arm aerates the ingredients in the bowl so that you can create light and smooth ice cream.
- **Double insulated walls:** The insulated walls of the Cuisinart Ice Cream maker contain a cooling liquid that speeds up the freezing process. The double-insulated walls keep the internal temperature even, so everything freezes up properly.
- **Space saver:** The Cuisinart Ice Cream Maker comes with space-saving designs. It has rubber feet that allow the machine to be stable while on use. The rubber feet also keep the machine from slipping thus it can be placed on any kind of surface. Moreover, it also comes with a cord storage that keeps the counter neat.

How to Use the Cuisinart Ice Cream Maker?

Using the Cuisinart Ice Cream Maker is no rocket science. As a matter of fact, this kitchen device does not come with many buttons–it only has the power button! This means that you only need to dump your ingredients, turn on the machine, and time the process to make your favorite frozen treats. But for additional information, below are general steps on how to use the Cuisinart Ice Cream Maker.

1. Place the detachable freezer bowl in the freezer for at least 2 hours.
2. Prepare the ingredients as indicated in the recipe. Make sure that the recipe yields not more than 1 ½-quarts or 4 cups.
3. Remove the freezer bowl from the freezer and place it on the center of the base. Make sure that you turn on the ice cream maker immediately as the bowl will begin to defrost and it may affect the time for the ingredients to become frozen.
4. Pace the mixing paddle in the freezer bowl and place the lid on the base. Rotate clockwise until the tabs on the lid lock in place.
5. Press the On/Off Switch to ON. This will make the freezer bowl turn.
6. Pour the ingredients through the ingredients spout. It is crucial to add the ingredients to the freezer bowl only after the unit is turned on.
7. Time your machine. Frozen desserts like ice cream are usually done within 20 minutes.
8. Transfer the dessert to an airtight container and freeze until ready to consume.
9. Never store the frozen desserts in the freezer bowl as the desserts might stick to its size causing damage to the bowl.

Recipe Tips

As you can make many frozen recipes with the Cuisinart Ice Cream maker, it is crucial that you know important recipe tips so that you can make delicious recipes at the comfort of your own home:

- Unlike commercial frozen treats, frozen treats made from home do not contain any preservatives and additives such as gums that impart commercial flavor and consistency of the dessert. To achieve firmer consistency, always transfer the frozen treats into airtight containers and store in the freezer to achieve desired consistency.
- For recipes that use precooked ingredients, make sure that such ingredients are chilled overnight before using or chilled over the ice bath. Putting in hot or warm ingredients may increase or raise the temperature inside the freezer bowl affecting the entire freezing process.
- Substitute low-fat creams such as half and half as well as non-dairy milk for heavy cream and whole milk. The higher the fat content, the creamier, and richer the desserts will be. If you use lower-fat substitute because you are health conscious, use the same volume of the substitute as you would with the original recipe.
- For recipes that use alcohol, add alcohol during the last two minutes of the freezing process. Adding the alcohol earlier may impede the freezing process.
- When making the sorbet, make sure that you use ripe fruits. The freezing process often reduces the sweetness of the fruit so that it tastes less sweet than what you will expect. If the fruit tastes tart, add sugar to the recipe.
- Never fill the freezer bowl higher than ¼-inch from the top of the freezer bowl. You have to take note that the volume of the ingredient doubles during the freezing process.
- When making more than one recipe at a time, make sure that the freezer bowl is completely frozen before each use. You can purchase additional freezer bowls for ease and convenience.
- Ingredients such as nuts, and chips should be added 5 minutes before the recipe is complete. Once the dessert thickens, add the ingredients gradually through the ingredient spout. Make sure that they should be chopped into smaller pieces and not larger than a chocolate chip.

Simple Ice Cream Recipes

Vanilla Ice Cream

Serves: 10
Cooking Time: 25 minutes

Ingredients:
- 1 cup cold whole milk
- ¾ cup granulated sugar
- 2 cups cold heavy cream
- 1 teaspoon vanilla extract

Directions:
1. Put ice water in a large mixing bowl. Place a small bowl on top of the large bowl with ice. Pour cold milk and sugar into the small bowl and whisk until the sugar is dissolved. Stir in the cream and vanilla. Stir to combine.
2. Place the cold freezer bowl in the Cuisinart Ice Cream Maker. Turn on the machine and pour in the mixture. Stop in 25 minutes until the mixture becomes soft and creamy.
3. Transfer into an air-tight container and freeze overnight.

Nutrition Information:
Calories per serving:135 ; Protein: 1.2g; Carbs: 11.3 g; Fat: 9g Sugar: 11.2g

Butter Pecan Ice Cream

Serves: 10
Cooking Time: 25 minutes

Ingredients:
- ½ cup unsalted butter
- 1 cup chopped pecan
- 1 teaspoon salt
- 1 cup ice cold whole milk
- ¾ cup granulated sugar
- 2 cups ice cold heavy cream
- 1 teaspoon pure vanilla extract

Directions:
1. Melt the butter in skillet and add the nuts and salt. Sauté over medium heat until the nuts are golden. Remove and strain the nuts. Reserve the butter for another use. Set aside the nuts. Allow the nuts to cool at least to room temperature.
2. Put ice water in a large mixing bowl. Place a small bowl on top of the large bowl with ice. Whisk in the milk and sugar until the sugar dissolves. Add the heavy cream and vanilla. Stir until combined.
3. Turn on the Cuisinart and pour the mixture in. Freeze for 25 minutes and add the nuts five minutes before the time ends.
4. Place the ice cream into a container and freeze overnight.

Nutrition Information:
Calories per serving: 281; Protein: 4.6g; Carbs:10.2 g; Fat: 25.4g Sugar: 9g

Chocolate Ice Cream

Serves: 10
Cooking Time: 25 minutes

Ingredients:
- 1 cup whole milk
- ½ cup granulated sugar
- 8 ounces semi-sweet chocolate, chopped into small chunks
- 2 cups ice cold heavy cream
- 1 teaspoon pure vanilla extract

Directions:
1. Warm milk in a stovetop under low heat until the temperature reads at 175^0F. Stir in the sugar and chocolate until dissolved. Turn off the heat and set aside in the fridge to cool.
2. Put ice water in a large mixing bowl. Place a small bowl on top of the large bowl with ice. Pour the milk chocolate mixture into the small bowl and add heavy cream and vanilla.
3. Turn on the Cuisinart and pour the mixture in. Freeze for 25 minutes before transferring into an air-tight container.
4. Freeze inside the fridge overnight before serving.

Nutrition Information:
Calories per serving:240 ; Protein: 2.1g; Carbs: 22.6g; Fat: 17g Sugar: 20.4g

Fresh Strawberry Ice Cream

Serves: 10
Cooking Time: 25 minutes

Ingredients:
- 1-pint strawberries, hulled and sliced
- 3 tablespoons lemon juice
- 1 cup white sugar, divided
- 1 cup ice cold whole milk
- 2 cups ice cold heavy cream
- 1 teaspoon vanilla extract

Directions:
1. Place half of the strawberries, lemon juice, and half of the sugar in a bowl. Macerate then strain to reserve the juice.
2. Chop the remaining strawberries. Set aside.
3. Put ice water in a large mixing bowl. Place a small bowl on top of the large bowl with ice.
4. Whisk together the whole milk, half of the sugar, heavy cream, and vanilla extract. Add the strawberry juice.
5. Turn on the Cuisinart and pour the mixture in. Freeze for 25 minutes. Five minutes before turning off the machine, add the chopped strawberries.
6. Transfer into air-tight containers and freeze overnight.

Nutrition Information:
Calories per serving: 178; Protein: 3.5g; Carbs: 14.5g; Fat: 12.2g Sugar: 12.4g

Mocha Ice Cream

Serves: 10
Cooking Time: 25 minutes

Ingredients:
- 1 cup ice cold whole milk
- ¼ cup granulated sugar
- 2 cups heavy cream
- 1 teaspoon vanilla extract
- 2 tablespoons instant coffee, dissolved in 3 tablespoons hot water

Directions:
1. Put ice water in a large mixing bowl. Place a small bowl on top of the large bowl with ice.
2. Pour the milk in the small bowl and add the sugar. Whisk until well-combined and the sugar dissolves. Add the rest of the ingredients and whisk.
3. Turn on the Cuisinart and pour the mixture in. Freeze for 25 minutes.
4. Transfer into air-tight containers and freeze overnight.

Nutrition Information:
Calories per serving:139 ; Protein: 3.4g; Carbs: 4.4g; Fat: 12.1g Sugar: 3.2g

Key Lime Ice Cream

Serves: 12
Cooking Time: 25 minutes

Ingredients:
- 1 ½ cups ice cold whole milk, divided
- 2/3 cup sugar
- 1 ¼ cups ice cold heavy whipping cream
- ½ cup key lime juice, freshly squeezed
- 2 tablespoons light corn syrup
- ¼ tablespoon salt

Directions:
1. Put ice water in a large mixing bowl. Place a small bowl on top of the large bowl with ice.
2. Pour in the milk and sugar until well-combined. Add the cream and whip until well combined.
3. Stir in the rest of the ingredients while whipping constantly.
4. Turn on the Cuisinart and pour the mixture in. Freeze for 25 minutes.
5. Transfer into air-tight containers and freeze overnight.

Nutrition Information:
Calories per serving: 96; Protein: 1.4g; Carbs: 11g; Fat: 5.6g Sugar: 10.2g

Vegan Ice Cream

Serves: 12
Cooking Time: 45 minutes

Ingredients:
- 2 13.5-ounce cans full-fat coconut milk
- ½ cup raw sugar
- 1 teaspoon vanilla extract
- 1 pinch xanthan gum
- ½ cup dark chocolate chips
- 1/3 cup roasted salted peanuts

Directions:
1. Pour in the coconut milk and sugar in a saucepan and whisk until well-combined. Add the vanilla and xanthan gum. Bring to a boil and whisk for 5 minutes.
2. Turn off the heat and allow to cool in the fridge for at least 6 hours.
3. Turn on the Cuisinart and pour the mixture in. Freeze for 45 minutes.
4. Add the chocolate chips and peanuts into the mixture 5 minutes before stopping the machine.
5. Transfer into air-tight containers and freeze overnight.

Nutrition Information:
Calories per serving: 361; Protein: 4.1g; Carbs: 27.3g; Fat: 28.6g Sugar: 23.4g

Peach Ice Cream

Serves: 10
Cooking Time: 45 minutes

Ingredients:
- 2 ripe peaches, peeled, pitted, and sliced
- 1 ½ cups ice cold whole milk
- 1 cup ice cold whipping cream
- 4 ounces cubed cream cheese, room temperature
- ½ cup sugar
- 2 tablespoons honey
- ½ teaspoon vanilla extract
- 1/8 teaspoon salt

Directions:
1. Put ice water in a large mixing bowl. Place a small bowl on top of the large bowl with ice.
2. Place the peaches in a blender and pulse until smooth.
3. Pour the peaches in the chilled bowl and add the milk, whipping cream, cream cheese, and sugar. Whisk until well combined and smooth. Add the honey, vanilla extract, and salt.
4. Turn on the Cuisinart and pour the mixture in. Freeze for 45 minutes.
5. Transfer into air-tight containers and freeze overnight.

Nutrition Information:
Calories per serving:176 ; Protein: 5.6g; Carbs: 17.6 g; Fat: 9.7g Sugar: 14.2g

Mocha Madness Ice Cream

Serves: 10
Cooking Time: 45 minutes

Ingredients:
- 2 tablespoons unsweetened cocoa
- 2 tablespoons espresso powder
- 1 cup ice cold whole milk
- ¾ cup sugar
- 2 cups ice cold heavy cream
- 8 Oreo cookies, broken into small pieces

Directions:
1. Place cocoa, espresso powder, half of the milk and sugar in a pan. Bring to a simmer until everything dissolves. Turn off the heat and set aside in the fridge to cool.
2. Put ice water in a large mixing bowl. Place a small bowl on top of the large bowl with ice.
3. Pour in milk, sugar, espresso powder, and cocoa in the chilled bowl. Whisk until well combined.
4. Turn on the Cuisinart and pour the mixture in. Freeze for 45 minutes.
5. Transfer into air-tight containers and freeze overnight.

Nutrition Information:
Calories per serving: 213; Protein: 4.2g; Carbs: 17.4g; Fat: 14.8g Sugar: 11.6g

Apricot Ice Cream

Serves: 10
Cooking Time: 45 minutes

Ingredients:
- 1 ½ tablespoons lemon zest
- ½ cup apricot, mashed
- 1 cup sugar
- 1 ½ cups ice cold whole milk
- 1 ½ cups cold whipping cream

Directions:
1. Put ice water in a large mixing bowl. Place a small bowl on top of the large bowl with ice.
2. To the small bowl, whisk together the lemon zest, mashed apricot, sugar, and milk. Whisk until well combined.
3. Add the whipping cream then whisk again to incorporate all ingredients.
4. Turn on the Cuisinart and pour the mixture in. Freeze for 45 minutes.
5. Transfer into air-tight containers and freeze overnight.

Nutrition Information:
Calories per serving: 143; Protein: 4.7g; Carbs: 16.5g; Fat: 6.8g Sugar: 14.2g

Rhubarb Swirl Ice Cream

Serves: 10
Cooking Time: 45 minutes

Ingredients:
- 4 stalks rhubarb, cut into ½ inch pieces
- 1 cup water
- ¾ cup sugar
- 1 cup ice cold whole milk
- ¾ cup sugar
- 1 ½ teaspoon pure vanilla extract
- A pinch of salt
- 2 cups cold heavy cream

Directions:
1. Place the rhubarb, water, and sugar in a saucepan and heat over high flame. Bring to a boil and cook while stirring constantly until the rhubarb will break down and turns into a jelly-like consistency. Set aside to cool.
2. Put ice water in a large mixing bowl. Place a small bowl on top of the large bowl with ice.
3. To the chilled small bowl, add the milk, sugar, vanilla, and salt. Whisk until well combined. Whisk in the heavy cream.
4. Turn on the Cuisinart and pour the mixture in. Freeze for 45 minutes.
5. Transfer into air-tight containers. Drizzle with the cooled rhubarb jelly and stir again.
6. Freeze overnight.

Nutrition Information:
Calories per serving: 190; Protein: 3.5g; Carbs: 17.4g; Fat: 12.1g Sugar: 15.7g

Blackberry Ice Cream

Serves: 10
Cooking Time: 45 minutes

Ingredients:
- 1 ½ cups blackberries, frozen or fresh
- ¾ cup ice cold whole milk
- ½ cup sugar
- A pinch of salt
- 1 ½ cup heavy cream, ice cold
- 1 ½ teaspoon vanilla

Directions:
1. Clean the blackberries by removing the stem and seeds. Mash to release the juice and pass through a sieve. Save the juice and set aside.
2. Put ice water in a large mixing bowl. Place a small bowl on top of the large bowl with ice.
3. Place the whole milk, sugar, and salt. Whisk to combine everything. Add the cream, vanilla, and blackberry juice. Stir to combined.
4. Turn on the Cuisinart and pour the mixture in. Freeze for 45 minutes.
5. Transfer into air-tight containers.
6. Freeze overnight.

Nutrition Information:
Calories per serving: 151; Protein: 3g; Carbs: 15g; Fat: 9.1g Sugar: 13.1g

Orange Creamsicle Ice Cream

Serves: 10
Cooking Time: 45 minutes

Ingredients:
- ¼ cup water
- Zest from 1 orange
- ½ cup orange juice
- 1 tablespoon arrowroot powder
- 1 cup ice cold whole milk
- ¾ cup granulated sugar
- 2 cups heavy cream
- A pinch of salt

Directions:
1. Place half of the ¼ cup water orange zest, orange juice, and arrowroot powder in a saucepan. Stir to combine everything. Bring to a boil until the mixture thickens. Set aside to cool.
2. Put ice water in a large mixing bowl. Place a small bowl on top of the large bowl with ice.
3. Add the milk and sugar. Whisk until well combined. Stir in the cooled orange mixture and whisk until well incorporated and the lumps are dissolved. Add the rest of the ingredients.
4. Turn on the Cuisinart and pour the mixture in. Freeze for 45 minutes.
5. Transfer into air-tight containers.
6. Freeze overnight.

Nutrition Information:
Calories per serving:164 ; Protein: 3.4g; Carbs: 11.1g; Fat: 12.1g Sugar: 9.1g

Pineapple Ice Cream

Serves: 6
Cooking Time: 45 minutes

Ingredients:
- 1 ½ cup pineapple juice
- 1 can crushed pineapple
- ½ cup heavy whipping cream

Directions:
1. Put ice water in a large mixing bowl. Place a small bowl on top of the large bowl with ice.
2. Place all ingredients in the small bowl. Whisk until well combined.
3. Turn on the Cuisinart and pour the mixture in. Freeze for 45 minutes.
4. Transfer into air-tight containers.
5. Freeze overnight.

Nutrition Information:

Calories per serving: 136; Protein: 1g; Carbs: 26g; Fat: 3.8g Sugar: 24g

Purple Taro Ice Cream

Serves: 10
Cooking Time: 1 hour 15 minutes

Ingredients:
- 1 cup purple taro, peeled and cubed
- 1 cup ice cold whole milk
- ¾ cup sugar
- 1 ½ cup ice cold heavy cream
- 2 tablespoons vanilla extract

Directions:
1. Place the purple taro in a saucepan and add enough water to cover the taro. Bring to a boil for 35 minutes or until soft. Drain to remove excess water. Mash the purple taro using fork and remove big lumps. Set aside to cool.
2. Put ice water in a large mixing bowl. Place a small bowl on top of the large bowl with ice.
3. Place the milk and sugar in the bowl and stir to dissolve the sugar. Add the mashed and cooled taro in the mixture. Add the heavy cream and vanilla. Stir to combine.
4. Turn on the Cuisinart and pour the mixture in. Freeze for 45 minutes.
5. Transfer into air-tight containers.
6. Freeze overnight.

Nutrition Information:
Calories per serving: 154; Protein: 3.3g; Carbs: 11.8 g; Fat: 9.9g Sugar: 8.3g

Eggless Pistachio Ice Cream

Serves: 10
Cooking Time: 45 minutes

Ingredients:
- 1 cup ice cold whole milk
- 1 cup sugar
- 2 cups ice cold heavy cream
- ½ teaspoon vanilla extract
- 1 cup pistachio nuts, chopped

Directions:
1. Put ice water in a large mixing bowl. Place a small bowl on top of the large bowl with ice.
2. Place the milk and sugar in the bowl and whisk to dissolve the sugar. Add the cream and vanilla extract.
3. Turn on the Cuisinart and pour the mixture in. Freeze for 45 minutes. Five minutes before the time, add the pistachio nuts.
4. Transfer into air-tight containers. Freeze overnight.

Nutrition Information:
Calories per serving:235 ; Protein: 5.8g; Carbs: 15.8g; Fat: 17.7g Sugar:11.5 g

Coconut Ice Cream

Serves: 10
Cooking Time: 45 minutes

Ingredients:
- 1 cup ice cold whole milk
- ½ cup sugar
- 14 ounces cream of coconut, approximately 1 ¾ cups
- 1 ½ cups heavy cream
- ¼ toasted coconut flakes

Directions:
1. Put ice water in a large mixing bowl. Place a small bowl on top of the large bowl with ice.
2. Place the milk and sugar in the bowl. Whisk to dissolve the sugar. Add the coconut cream and heavy cream.
3. Turn on the Cuisinart and pour the mixture in. Freeze for 45 minutes. Five minutes before the time, add the toasted coconut flakes.
4. Transfer into air-tight containers. Freeze overnight.

Nutrition Information:
Calories per serving: 387; Protein: 2g; Carbs: 37g; Fat: 26g Sugar: 35g

Cinnamon Ice Cream

Serves: 10
Cooking Time: 45 minutes

Ingredients:
- 2 cups heavy cream
- 1 cup half and half
- ½ cup sugar
- ¼ cup brown sugar
- 1 teaspoon vanilla extract
- 1 tablespoon cinnamon
- A pinch of salt

Directions:
1. Put ice water in a large mixing bowl. Place a small bowl on top of the large bowl with ice.
2. Pour all ingredients in the bowl. Whisk until well-combined.
3. Turn on the Cuisinart and pour the mixture in. Freeze for 45 minutes.
4. Transfer into air-tight containers. Freeze overnight.

Nutrition Information:
Calories per serving: 140; Protein: 1.1g; Carbs: 13.8 g; Fat: 9.2g Sugar: 12.1g

Coffee Toffee Ice Cream

Serves: 10
Cooking Time: 45 minutes

Ingredients:
- 1 ½ cups ice cold whole milk
- 1 1/8 cups granulated sugar
- 3 cups ice cold heavy cream
- 1 ½ tablespoons vanilla extract
- 4 tablespoons Instant Espresso Powder
- 12 ounces min chocolate bars, chopped

Directions:
1. Put ice water in a large mixing bowl. Place a small bowl on top of the large bowl with ice.
2. Place the milk and sugar in the bowl. Whisk to dissolve the sugar. Add the cream, vanilla extract, and espresso powder. Stir to combine everything.
3. Turn on the Cuisinart and pour the mixture in. Freeze for 45 minutes. Five minutes before the time, add the chopped chocolate bars.
4. Transfer into air-tight containers. Freeze overnight.

Nutrition Information:
Calories per serving: 358; Protein: 6.6g; Carbs: 37.4g; Fat: 21.6g Sugar: 21g

Banana Pudding Ice Cream

Serves: 8
Cooking Time: 25 minutes

Ingredients:
- 1 ½ cups half and half
- ½ cup packed brown sugar
- ½ cup white sugar
- 1/8 teaspoon salt
- 1 cup heavy whipping cream
- 1 ½ teaspoon vanilla extract
- 2 ripe bananas, mashed
- 1 cup crushed wafers, any brand

Directions:
1. Place the half and half, brown sugar, white sugar, and salt in a saucepan. Bring to a boil until the sugar dissolves. Turn off the heat and place in the fridge to cool.
2. Put ice water in a large mixing bowl. Place a small bowl on top of the large bowl with ice.
3. Place the cooled milk mixture in the bowl and add the whipping cream, vanilla extract, and bananas. Whisk to combine everything.
4. Turn on the Cuisinart and pour the mixture in. Freeze for 25 minutes. Five minutes before the time, add the wafers.
5. Transfer into air-tight containers. Freeze overnight.

Nutrition Information:
Calories per serving:196 ; Protein: 2.6g; Carbs: 28.4g; Fat: 8.8g Sugar: 22.1g

Custard Style Ice Cream Recipes

Vanilla Frozen Custard

Serves: 6
Cooking Time: 30 minutes

Ingredients:
- 2 cups heavy cream
- 1 cup whole milk
- 2/3 cup granulated sugar
- A pinch of salt
- 6 large egg yolks
- 2 teaspoons vanilla extract

Directions:
1. Add the cream, milk, sugar, and salt in a saucepan and heat over medium low flame. Simmer for 3 minutes or until the sugar dissolves.
2. Remove from the heat.
3. In a bowl, whisk in the egg yolks. Drizzle ½ cup of the warm milk into the egg yolks while whisking constantly to form a smooth mixture. Whisk the egg mixture back into the pot and add vanilla.
4. Turn on the heat to medium low and cook until the mixture starts to thicken. Constantly stir while cooking.
5. Turn off the heat and strain the mixture to remove lumps. Allow the milk to cool at room temperature. Place in the fridge to chill for 2 hours.
6. Turn on the Cuisinart and pour the mixture in. Churn for 15 minutes.
7. Transfer to an airtight container and place in the fridge to completely cool.

Nutrition Information:
Calories per serving: 443; Protein: 5g; Carbs: 27 g; Fat: 35g Sugar: 24g

Basic Custard Ice Cream with Sea Salt

Serves: 10
Cooking Time: 30 minutes

Ingredients:
- 3 cups whole milk
- 1 cup sugar
- 8 egg yolks
- 1 teaspoon vanilla
- A pinch of coarse sea salt

Directions:
1. Add the milk and sugar in a saucepan and heat over medium low flame. Simmer for 3 minutes or until the sugar dissolves. Remove from the heat.
2. In a bowl, whisk in the egg yolks. Drizzle ½ cup of the warm milk into the egg yolks while whisking constantly to form a smooth mixture. Whisk the egg mixture back into the pot.
3. Turn on the heat to medium low and cook until the mixture starts to thicken. Constantly stir while cooking.
4. Turn off the heat and strain the mixture to remove lumps. Allow the milk to cool at room temperature. Place in the fridge to chill for 2 hours.
5. Turn on the Cuisinart and pour the mixture in. Churn for 15 minutes.
6. Transfer to an airtight container and sprinkle with sea salt on top.
7. Place in the fridge to completely cool.

Nutrition Information:
Calories per serving: 50; Protein: 1.42g; Carbs: 6.7g; Fat: 2g Sugar: 5g

Custard Chocolate Ice Cream

Serves: 10
Cooking Time: 30 minutes

Ingredients:
- 1/3 cup unsweetened cocoa powder
- 2 cups heavy whipping cream
- 1 cup whole milk
- ¾ cup sugar
- 6 large egg yolks
- A pinch of salt
- 1 ½ teaspoons vanilla extract

Directions:
1. Add the coca powder, cream, milk and sugar in a saucepan and heat over medium low flame. Simmer for 3 minutes or until the sugar dissolves. Remove from the heat.
2. In a bowl, whisk in the egg yolks. Drizzle ½ cup of the warm milk into the egg yolks while whisking constantly to form a smooth mixture. Whisk the egg mixture back into the pot. Add the salt and vanilla.
3. Turn on the heat to medium low and cook until the mixture starts to thicken. Constantly stir while cooking.
4. Turn off the heat and strain the mixture to remove lumps. Allow the milk to cool at room temperature. Place in the fridge to chill for 2 hours.
5. Turn on the Cuisinart and pour the mixture in. Churn for 15 minutes.
6. Transfer to an airtight container.
7. Place in the fridge to completely cool.

Nutrition Information:
Calories per serving: 175; Protein: 3.5g; Carbs: 13.4g; Fat: 12.7g Sugar: 11.3g

Custard Cantaloupe Ice Cream

Serves: 10
Cooking Time: 30 minutes

Ingredients:
- 3 cups whole milk
- 1 cup sugar
- 8 egg yolks
- A pinch of salt
- 1 cup cantaloupe, seeds removed and mashed

Directions:
1. Add the milk and sugar in a saucepan and heat over medium low flame. Simmer for 3 minutes or until the sugar dissolves. Remove from the heat.
2. In a bowl, whisk in the egg yolks. Drizzle ½ cup of the warm milk into the egg yolks while whisking constantly to form a smooth mixture. Whisk the egg mixture back into the pot. Add the salt.
3. Turn on the heat to medium low and cook until the mixture starts to thicken. Constantly stir while cooking.
4. Turn off the heat and strain the mixture to remove lumps. Allow the milk to cool at room temperature. Place in the fridge to chill for 2 hours.
5. Turn on the Cuisinart and pour the mixture in. Churn for 15 minutes.
6. Five minutes before the time ends, add the mashed cantaloupe.
7. Transfer to an airtight container.
8. Place in the fridge to completely cool.

Nutrition Information:
Calories per serving:155 ; Protein: 4.5g; Carbs: 21.4g; Fat: 5.9g Sugar: 20.1g

Turmeric Ice Cream

Serves: 10
Cooking Time: 30 minutes

Ingredients:
- 3 cups whole milk
- 1 cup sugar
- 2 tablespoons turmeric powder
- 8 egg yolks
- A pinch of salt

Directions:
1. Add the milk, sugar, and turmeric powder in a saucepan and heat over medium low flame. Simmer for 3 minutes or until the sugar dissolves. Remove from the heat.
2. In a bowl, whisk in the egg yolks. Drizzle ½ cup of the warm milk into the egg yolks while whisking constantly to form a smooth mixture. Whisk the egg mixture back into the pot. Add the salt.
3. Turn on the heat to medium low and cook until the mixture starts to thicken. Constantly stir while cooking.
4. Turn off the heat and strain the mixture to remove lumps. Allow the milk to cool at room temperature. Place in the fridge to chill for 2 hours.
5. Turn on the Cuisinart and pour the mixture in. Churn for 15 minutes.
6. Transfer to an airtight container.
7. Place in the fridge to completely cool.

Nutrition Information:
Calories per serving:155 ; Protein: 5g; Carbs: 22g; Fat: 5g Sugar: 19g

Mango Ice Cream

Serves: 10
Cooking Time: 15 minutes

Ingredients:
- 3 cups whole milk
- 1 cup sugar
- 8 egg yolks
- A pinch of salt
- ¼ cup mango puree
- 3 tablespoons dried mango, chopped

Directions:
1. Add the milk and sugar in a saucepan and heat over medium low flame. Simmer for 3 minutes or until the sugar dissolves. Remove from the heat.
2. In a bowl, whisk in the egg yolks. Drizzle ½ cup of the warm milk into the egg yolks while whisking constantly to form a smooth mixture. Whisk the egg mixture back into the pot. Add the salt.
3. Turn on the heat to medium low and cook until the mixture starts to thicken. Constantly stir while cooking. Add the mango puree last.
4. Turn off the heat and strain the mixture to remove lumps. Allow the milk to cool at room temperature. Place in the fridge to chill for 2 hours.
5. Turn on the Cuisinart and pour the mixture in. Churn for 15 minutes.
6. Five minutes before the time ends, add the dried mango.
7. Transfer to an airtight container.
8. Place in the fridge to completely cool.

Nutrition Information:
Calories per serving:154 ; Protein: 4.3g; Carbs: 21.2g; Fat: 5.8g Sugar: 20.4g

Rocky Road Frozen Custard Ice Cream

Serves: 12
Cooking Time: 30 minutes

Ingredients:
- 1 cup whole milk
- 2 cups heavy cream
- ¾ cup sugar
- ½ teaspoon salt
- 2 tablespoons unsweetened cocoa powder
- ½ teaspoon ground cinnamon
- 3 egg yolks
- 2 ounces chocolate bar, chopped
- 1 cup mini marshmallows
- ½ cup toasted pecans

Directions:
1. Add the milk, cream, sugar, and salt in a saucepan and heat over medium low flame. Simmer for 3 minutes or until the sugar dissolves. Add the cocoa powder and cinnamon. Stir for another minute. Remove from the heat.
2. In a bowl, whisk in the egg yolks. Drizzle ½ cup of the warm milk into the egg yolks while whisking constantly to form a smooth mixture. Whisk the egg mixture back into the pot.
3. Turn on the heat to medium low and cook until the mixture starts to thicken. Constantly stir while cooking.
4. Turn off the heat and strain the mixture to remove lumps. Allow the milk to cool at room temperature. Place in the fridge to chill for 2 hours.
5. Turn on the Cuisinart and pour the mixture in. Churn for 15 minutes.
6. Five minutes before the time ends, add the chopped chocolate, marshmallows, and pecans.
7. Transfer to an airtight container.
8. Place in the fridge to completely cool.

Nutrition Information:
Calories per serving: 189; Protein: 2.6g; Carbs: 13.8g; Fat: 14.4g Sugar: 11.3g

Honey Ice Cream

Serves: 12
Cooking Time: 30 minutes

Ingredients:
- 1 ½ cups heavy cream
- 1 ½ cups whole milk
- ½ cup honey
- ½ teaspoon salt
- 4 large egg yolks
- 1 ½ teaspoon vanilla extract

Directions:
1. Add the cream, milk, honey, and salt in a saucepan and heat over medium low flame. Simmer for 3 minutes or until the sugar dissolves.
2. In a bowl, whisk in the egg yolks. Drizzle ½ cup of the warm milk into the egg yolks while whisking constantly to form a smooth mixture. Whisk the egg mixture back into the pot.
3. Turn on the heat to medium low and cook until the mixture starts to thicken. Constantly stir while cooking.
4. Turn off the heat and strain the mixture to remove lumps. Allow the milk to cool at room temperature. Place in the fridge to chill for 2 hours.
5. Turn on the Cuisinart and pour the mixture in. Churn for 15 minutes.
6. Transfer to an airtight container.
7. Place in the fridge to completely cool.

Nutrition Information:
Calories per serving:142 ; Protein: 2.2g; Carbs: 16.3g; Fat: 8g Sugar: 16g

Pumpkin Custard Ice Cream

Serves: 6   Cooking Time: 30 minutes

Ingredients:
- 2 cups heavy cream
- 2 cups milk
- ¼ cup granulated sugar
- ¾ cup brown sugar
- 1/8 teaspoon salt
- 3 egg yolk
- 1 teaspoon cinnamon
- ¼ teaspoon grated nutmeg
- 1/8 teaspoon ground cloves
- 1/8 teaspoon ground ginger
- 1 tablespoon vanilla extract
- 1 cup canned pumpkin, mashed

Directions:
1. Add the cream, milk, sugar, and salt in a saucepan and heat over medium low flame. Simmer for 3 minutes or until the sugar dissolves. Remove from the stove.
2. In a bowl, whisk in the egg yolks. Drizzle ½ cup of the warm milk into the egg yolks while whisking constantly to form a smooth mixture. Whisk the egg mixture back into the pot. Add the cinnamon, nutmeg, cloves, ginger, and vanilla.
3. Turn on the heat to medium low and cook until the mixture starts to thicken. Constantly stir while cooking.
4. Turn off the heat and strain the mixture to remove lumps. Allow the milk to cool at room temperature. Place in the fridge to chill for 2 hours.
5. Turn on the Cuisinart and pour the mixture in. Add the mashed pumpkin. Churn for 15 minutes.
6. Transfer to an airtight container.
7. Place in the fridge to completely cool.

Nutrition Information:
Calories per serving:457 ; Protein: 10.7g; Carbs: 40g; Fat: 29g Sugar: 47g

Custard Cream Gelato

Serves: 20
Cooking Time: 30 minutes

Ingredients:
- 6 cups whole milk
- 1 1/3 cups sugar
- 12 egg yolks
- 1 medium lemon juice

Directions:
1. Add the milk and sugar in a saucepan and heat over medium low flame. Simmer for 3 minutes or until the sugar dissolves. Remove from the stove.
2. In a bowl, whisk in the egg yolks. Drizzle ½ cup of the warm milk into the egg yolks while whisking constantly to form a smooth mixture. Whisk the egg mixture back into the pot. Add the lemon juice while stirring constantly.
3. Turn on the heat to medium low and cook until the mixture starts to thicken. Constantly stir while cooking.
4. Turn off the heat and strain the mixture to remove lumps. Allow the milk to cool at room temperature. Place in the fridge to chill for 2 hours.
5. Turn on the Cuisinart and pour the mixture in. Churn for 15 minutes.
6. Transfer to an airtight container.
7. Place in the fridge to completely cool.

Nutrition Information:
Calories per serving:125 ; Protein: 3.8g; Carbs: 16.6g; Fat: 4.9g Sugar: 16g

Thermomix Licorice Ice Cream

Serves: 12
Cooking Time: 30 minutes

Ingredients:
- 3 cups heavy cream
- 2 cups whole milk
- ½ cup sugar
- A pinch of salt
- 6 egg yolks
- ½ teaspoon black food coloring
- ¼ cup soft licorice, chopped

Directions:
1. Add the cream, milk, sugar, and salt in a saucepan and heat over medium low flame. Simmer for 3 minutes or until the sugar dissolves. Remove from the stove.
2. In a bowl, whisk in the egg yolks. Drizzle ½ cup of the warm milk into the egg yolks while whisking constantly to form a smooth mixture. Whisk the egg mixture back into the pot. Add the black food coloring and licorice.
3. Turn on the heat to medium low and cook until the mixture starts to thicken. Constantly stir while cooking.
4. Turn off the heat and strain the mixture to remove lumps. Allow the milk to cool at room temperature. Place in the fridge to chill for 2 hours.
5. Turn on the Cuisinart and pour the mixture in. Churn for 15 minutes.
6. Transfer to an airtight container.
7. Place in the fridge to completely cool.

Nutrition Information:
Calories per serving:342 ; Protein: 3g; Carbs: 32g; Fat: 22g Sugar: 22g

Barbados Custard Ice Cream

Serves: 12
Cooking Time: 30 minutes

Ingredients:
- 2 cups whole milk
- ½ cup sugar
- ¼ cup light brown sugar
- A pinch of salt
- 1 vanilla pod, scraped
- 6 egg yolks
- ½ cup crème fraiche
- 1 tablespoon dark rum

Directions:
1. Add the milk, sugar, and salt in a saucepan and heat over medium low flame. Simmer for 3 minutes or until the sugar dissolves. Remove from the stove.
2. In a bowl, whisk in the egg yolks. Drizzle ½ cup of the warm milk into the egg yolks while whisking constantly to form a smooth mixture. Whisk the egg mixture back into the pot. Add the vanilla, crème fraiche, and rum.
3. Turn on the heat to medium low and cook until the mixture starts to thicken. Constantly stir while cooking.
4. Turn off the heat and strain the mixture to remove lumps. Allow to cool at room temperature. Place in the fridge to chill for 2 hours.
5. Turn on the Cuisinart and pour the mixture in. Churn for 15 minutes.
6. Transfer to an airtight container.
7. Place in the fridge to completely cool.

Nutrition Information:
Calories per serving: 103; Protein: 2.7g; Carbs: 10.2g; Fat: 5.5g Sugar: 9.6g

Strawberry Matcha Custard Ice Cream

Serves: 10
Cooking Time: 30 minutes

Ingredients:
- 3 cups heavy cream
- 1 cup milk
- ¾ cup sugar
- A pinch of salt
- 1 vanilla bean, scraped
- 6 egg yolks
- ½ cup chopped strawberries
- 3 tablespoons matcha or green tea powder

Directions:
1. Add the cream, milk, sugar, and salt in a saucepan and heat over medium low flame. Simmer for 3 minutes or until the sugar dissolves. Stir in the vanilla bean paste. Remove from the stove.
2. In a bowl, whisk in the egg yolks. Drizzle ½ cup of the warm milk into the egg yolks while whisking constantly to form a smooth mixture. Whisk the egg mixture back into the pot.
3. Turn on the heat to medium low and cook until the mixture starts to thicken. Constantly stir while cooking.
4. Turn off the heat and strain the mixture to remove lumps. Allow to cool at room temperature. Place in the fridge to chill for 2 hours.
5. Turn on the Cuisinart and pour the mixture in. Add the chopped strawberries. Churn for 15 minutes.
6. Transfer to an airtight container. Sprinkle with matcha powder on top.
7. Place in the fridge to completely cool.

Nutrition Information:
Calories per serving:204 ; Protein: 3.2g; Carbs: 10.6g; Fat: 16.9g Sugar: 10g

Banana Custard Ice Cream

Serves: 8
Cooking Time: 30 minutes

Ingredients:
- 2 cups heavy cream
- 2 cups half and half
- 5 tablespoons evaporated milk
- 1 ¼ cups granulated sugar
- ¼ teaspoon salt
- 4 egg yolks, beaten
- 1 cup mashed ripe bananas
- 2 tablespoons roasted peanuts, chopped

Directions:
1. Add the cream, half and half, milk, sugar, and salt in a saucepan and heat over medium low flame. Simmer for 3 minutes or until the sugar dissolves. Remove from the stove.
2. In a bowl, whisk in the egg yolks. Drizzle ½ cup of the warm milk into the egg yolks while whisking constantly to form a smooth mixture. Whisk the egg mixture back into the pot.
3. Turn on the heat to medium low and cook until the mixture starts to thicken. Constantly stir while cooking.
4. Turn off the heat and strain the mixture to remove lumps. Allow to cool at room temperature. Place in the fridge to chill for 2 hours.
5. Turn on the Cuisinart and pour the mixture in. Add the mashed bananas. Churn for 15 minutes.
6. Five minutes before the time ends, add the roasted peanuts.
7. Transfer to an airtight container.
8. Place in the fridge to completely cool.

Nutrition Information:
Calories per serving: 298; Protein: 5.4g; Carbs: 35g; Fat:16.2 g Sugar: 26g

Cookies and Cream Ice Cream

Serves: 10
Cooking Time: 30 minutes

Ingredients:
- 2 cups heavy cream
- 1 cup whole milk
- ¾ cup sugar
- 2 teaspoons vanilla extract
- A pinch of salt
- 6 egg yolks
- 1 cup Oreo cookies, chopped

Directions:
1. Add the cream, milk, sugar, vanilla extract, and salt in a saucepan and heat over medium low flame. Simmer for 3 minutes or until the sugar dissolves. Remove from the stove.
2. In a bowl, whisk in the egg yolks. Drizzle ½ cup of the warm milk into the egg yolks while whisking constantly to form a smooth mixture. Whisk the egg mixture back into the pot.
3. Turn on the heat to medium low and cook until the mixture starts to thicken. Constantly stir while cooking.
4. Turn off the heat and strain the mixture to remove lumps. Allow to cool at room temperature. Place in the fridge to chill for 2 hours.
5. Turn on the Cuisinart and pour the mixture in. Churn for 15 minutes.
6. Five minutes before the time ends, add the chopped Oreo cookies.
7. Transfer to an airtight container.
8. Place in the fridge to completely cool.

Nutrition Information:
Calories per serving:219 ; Protein: 4g; Carbs: 20 g; Fat: 13.9g Sugar: 15.5g

Pralines and Cream Custard Ice Cream

Serves: 8
Cooking Time: 30 minutes

Ingredients:
- 2 cups heavy cream
- 1 ½ cups half and half
- ¾ cup sugar
- 1 teaspoon vanilla extract
- ¼ teaspoon salt
- 4 egg yolks
- 1 cup caramel sauce
- 1 cup praline pecans

Directions:
1. Add the cream, milk, sugar, vanilla extract, and salt in a saucepan and heat over medium low flame. Simmer for 3 minutes or until the sugar dissolves. Remove from the stove.
2. In a bowl, whisk in the egg yolks. Drizzle ½ cup of the warm milk into the egg yolks while whisking constantly to form a smooth mixture. Whisk the egg mixture back into the pot.
3. Turn on the heat to medium low and cook until the mixture starts to thicken. Constantly stir while cooking.
4. Turn off the heat and strain the mixture to remove lumps. Allow to cool at room temperature. Place in the fridge to chill for 2 hours.
5. Turn on the Cuisinart and pour the mixture in. Churn for 15 minutes.
6. Five minutes before the time ends, add the caramel sauce and pecans.
7. Transfer to an airtight container.
8. Place in the fridge to completely cool.

Nutrition Information:
Calories per serving: 474; Protein: 4g; Carbs: 46g; Fat: 32g Sugar: 24g

Double Espresso Ice Cream

Serves: 10
Cooking Time: 30 minutes

Ingredients:
- 2 cups half and half
- 1 ½ cups heavy cream
- 14 ounces sweetened condensed milk
- 2 tablespoons espresso powder
- 6 egg yolks
- ¼ cup chocolate-covered espresso beans, chopped

Directions:
1. Add the half and half, cream, condensed milk, and espresso powder in a saucepan and heat over medium low flame. Simmer for 3 minutes. Remove from the stove.
2. In a bowl, whisk in the egg yolks. Drizzle ½ cup of the warm milk into the egg yolks while whisking constantly to form a smooth mixture. Whisk the egg mixture back into the pot.
3. Turn on the heat to medium low and cook until the mixture starts to thicken. Constantly stir while cooking.
4. Turn off the heat and strain the mixture to remove lumps. Allow to cool at room temperature. Place in the fridge to chill for 2 hours.
5. Turn on the Cuisinart and pour the mixture in. Churn for 15 minutes.
6. Five minutes before the time ends, add the chocolate-covered espresso beans.
7. Transfer to an airtight container.
8. Place in the fridge to completely cool.

Nutrition Information:
Calories per serving:166 ; Protein: 4.8g; Carbs: 9.2g; Fat: 12.4g Sugar: 5.6g

Nutella Ice Cream

Serves: 10
Cooking Time: 30 minutes

Ingredients:
- 2 cups heavy cream
- 1 cup whole milk
- 2/3 cup granulated sugar
- 1 teaspoon salt
- 6 egg yolks
- ½ cup Nutella
- 1 teaspoon vanilla extract

Directions:
1. Add the cream, milk, sugar, and salt in a saucepan and heat over medium low flame. Simmer for 3 minutes. Remove from the stove.
2. In a bowl, whisk in the egg yolks. Drizzle ½ cup of the warm milk into the egg yolks while whisking constantly to form a smooth mixture. Whisk the egg mixture back into the pot.
3. Turn on the heat to medium low and cook until the mixture starts to thicken. Constantly stir while cooking. Add Nutella and vanilla.
4. Turn off the heat and strain the mixture to remove lumps. Allow to cool at room temperature. Place in the fridge to chill for 2 hours.
5. Turn on the Cuisinart and pour the mixture in. Churn for 15 minutes.
6. Transfer to an airtight container.
7. Place in the fridge to completely cool.

Nutrition Information:
Calories per serving: 219; Protein: 3.4g; Carbs: 17.4g; Fat: 15.3g Sugar: 15.8g

Malted Milk Chocolate Ice Cream

Serves: 8
Cooking Time: 25 minutes

Ingredients:
- 1 ¾ cups heavy cream
- 1 cup whole milk
- 2/3 cup malted milk powder
- ½ cup sugar
- A pinch of salt
- 6 egg yolks
- 6 ounces milk chocolate, chopped
- ½ cup mini Cadbury eggs, chopped

Directions:
1. Add the cream, milk, sugar, and salt in a saucepan and heat over medium low flame. Simmer for 3 minutes. Remove from the stove.
2. In a bowl, whisk in the egg yolks. Drizzle ½ cup of the warm milk into the egg yolks while whisking constantly to form a smooth mixture. Whisk the egg mixture back into the pot.
3. Turn on the heat to medium low and cook until the mixture starts to thicken. Constantly stir while cooking.
4. Turn off the heat and strain the mixture to remove lumps. Allow to cool at room temperature. Place in the fridge to chill for 2 hours.
5. Turn on the Cuisinart and pour the mixture in. Churn for 15 minutes.
6. Before the churning time ends, add the chopped milk chocolate and Cadbury eggs.
7. Transfer to an airtight container.
8. Place in the fridge to completely cool.

Nutrition Information:
Calories per serving: 210; Protein: 5g; Carbs: 22g; Fat: 12g Sugar: 17g

Dark Chocolate Cheery Custard Ice Cream

Serves: 12
Cooking Time: 30 minutes

Ingredients:
- 1 cup whole milk
- 2 cups heavy cream
- 1 cup granulated sugar
- A pinch of salt
- 6 egg yolks
- 2 teaspoons vanilla extract
- ½ cup cherries, pitted and chopped
- ½ cup dark chocolate chips, shaved

Directions:
1. Add the milk, cream, sugar, and salt in a saucepan and heat over medium low flame. Simmer for 3 minutes. Remove from the stove.
2. In a bowl, whisk in the egg yolks. Drizzle ½ cup of the warm milk into the egg yolks while whisking constantly to form a smooth mixture. Whisk the egg mixture back into the pot. Add the vanilla extract.
3. Turn on the heat to medium low and cook until the mixture starts to thicken. Constantly stir while cooking.
4. Turn off the heat and strain the mixture to remove lumps. Allow to cool at room temperature. Place in the fridge to chill for 2 hours.
5. Turn on the Cuisinart and pour the mixture in. Churn for 15 minutes.
6. Before the churning time ends, add the cherries and chocolate shavings.
7. Transfer to an airtight container.
8. Place in the fridge to completely cool.

Nutrition Information:
Calories per serving:196 ; Protein: 2.8g; Carbs: 18.1g; Fat: 12.6g Sugar: 14.8g

Frozen Yogurt Recipes

Healthy Greek Frozen Yogurt

Serves: 5
Cooking Time: 10 minutes

Ingredients:
- 4 cups frozen fruit of your choice
- ½ cup plain Greek yogurt
- 2 teaspoons vanilla extract
- 3 tablespoons honey

Directions:
1. Place all ingredients in a food processor. Pulse until smooth.
2. Turn on the Cuisinart and pour in the mixture.
3. Churn for 10 minutes.
4. Transfer in an airtight container and freeze overnight.

Nutrition Information:
Calories per serving: 200; Protein: 2.9g; Carbs: 48.8g; Fat: 0.2g Sugar: 47g

Strawberry Vanilla Frozen Yogurt

Serves: 6
Cooking Time: 10 minutes

Ingredients:
- 3 cups non-fat Greek yogurt
- 2/3 cup white sugar
- 1 teaspoon vanilla extract
- 1 cup strawberries, hulled

Directions:
1. Place all ingredients in a food processor. Pulse until smooth.
2. Turn on the Cuisinart and pour in the mixture.
3. Churn for 10 minutes.
4. Transfer in an airtight container and freeze overnight.

Nutrition Information:
Calories per serving: 124; Protein: 9.2g; Carbs: 21.2g; Fat: 0.3g Sugar: 19.8g

Frozen Cantaloupe Yogurt

Serves: 6
Cooking Time: 10 minutes

Ingredients:
- 3 cups non-fat Greek yogurt
- 2/3 cup white sugar
- 1teaspoon vanilla extract
- 1 cup cantaloupe flesh

Directions:
1. Place all ingredients in a food processor. Pulse until smooth.
2. Turn on the Cuisinart and pour in the mixture.
3. Churn for 10 minutes.
4. Transfer in an airtight container and freeze overnight.

Nutrition Information:
Calories per serving: 126; Protein: 9.3g; Carbs: 21.7g; Fat: 0.3g Sugar: 20g

Blueberry Frozen Yogurt

Serves: 6
Cooking Time: 10 minutes

Ingredients:
- 2 ½ cups blueberries, fresh or frozen
- 2/3 cup honey
- 1 small lemon, zested and juiced
- ¼ teaspoon salt
- 2 cups full fat yogurt, chilled

Directions:
1. Place all ingredients in a food processor. Pulse until smooth.
2. Turn on the Cuisinart and pour in the mixture.
3. Churn for 10 minutes.
4. Transfer in an airtight container and freeze overnight.

Nutrition Information:

Calories per serving: 262; Protein:5.12 g; Carbs: 61g; Fat: 1.6g Sugar: 58.9g

Chocolate Frozen Yogurt

Serves: 5
Cooking Time: 10 minutes

Ingredients:
- 4 cups plain and unsweetened yogurt
- ½ cup cane sugar
- ¼ cup cocoa powder
- 1 teaspoon vanilla extract

Directions:
1. Place all ingredients in a food processor and pulse until smooth.
2. Turn on the Cuisinart and pour in the mixture.
3. Churn for 10 minutes.
4. Transfer in an airtight container and freeze overnight.

Nutrition Information:
Calories per serving:150 ; Protein: 7.6g; Carbs: 16.7g; Fat: 6.9g Sugar: 14g

Peach Frozen Yogurt

Serves: 5
Cooking Time: 10 minutes

Ingredients:
- 4 cups fresh peaches
- 3 tablespoons honey
- ½ cup plain Greek yogurt
- 1 teaspoon vanilla extract

Directions:
1. Place all ingredients in a food processor and pulse until smooth.
2. Turn on the Cuisinart and pour in the mixture.
3. Churn for 10 minutes.
4. Transfer in an airtight container and freeze overnight.

Nutrition Information:
Calories per serving: 109; Protein: 3g; Carbs: 24g; Fat: 3g Sugar: 23g

Tart Frozen Yogurt

Serves: 4
Cooking Time: 10 minutes

Ingredients:
- 2 cups plain yogurt
- 2 cups plain Greek yogurt
- ¾ cup sugar
- 2 tablespoons honey
- Fruits for topping

Directions:
1. Place the yogurt, sugar, and honey in a bowl. Whisk to combine everything. Place in the fridge to chill.
2. Turn on the Cuisinart and pour in the mixture.
3. Churn for 10 minutes.
4. Transfer in an airtight container and freeze overnight.
5. Top with your favorite fruit before serving.

Nutrition Information:
Calories per serving: 362; Protein: 21g; Carbs: 61g; Fat: 3g Sugar: 60g

Strawberry Basil Frozen Yogurt

Serves: 6
Cooking Time: 10 minutes

Ingredients:
- 1-pound strawberries, hulled
- 1 lemon, zested and juiced
- ½ cup sugar
- ¼ cup fresh basil leaves
- 1 ½ cups whole Greek yogurt
- 1 tablespoon honey

Directions:
1. Place the strawberries, lemon zest, juice, sugar, and basil leaves in a food processor. Pulse until smooth.
2. Place the mixture in a bowl and add the yogurt and honey. Whisk until combined. Chill in the fridge.
3. Turn on the Cuisinart and pour in the mixture.
4. Churn for 10 minutes.
5. Transfer in an airtight container and freeze overnight.

Nutrition Information:
Calories per serving:106 ; Protein: 2.7g; Carbs: 20.4g; Fat: 2.2g Sugar: 17.8g

Neapolitan Frozen Yogurt

Serves: 10
Cooking Time: 10 minutes

Ingredients:
- 1 cup cherries, pitted
- ½ cup icing sugar
- 1 lemon, juiced
- 2 cups plain Greek yogurt
- ½ cup frozen mango chunks
- 2 tablespoons honey
- ¼ cup frozen blueberries
- Mint leaves for garnish

Directions:
1. Place the cherries, icing sugar, and lemon juice in a food processor. Pulse until smooth.
2. Place in a bowl and add the yogurt. Allow to chill in the fridge for 30 minutes.
3. Turn on the Cuisinart and pour in the mixture.
4. Churn for 10 minutes.
5. Five minutes before churning ends, add the mango, honey, and blueberries.
6. Transfer in an airtight container and freeze overnight.
7. Serve with mint.

Nutrition Information:
Calories per serving: 66; Protein: 2.1g; Carbs: 10.9g; Fat: 2g Sugar: 9.4g

Dulce De Leche Frozen Yogurt

Serves: 8
Cooking Time: 10 minutes

Ingredients:
- 1 ½ cups plain whole milk yogurt
- 1 cup commercial Dulce de Leche
- 1 cup heavy cream
- 1/8 teaspoon salt
- ½ teaspoon vanilla extract

Directions:
1. Place all ingredients in a chilled bowl. Whisk until well-combined.
2. Turn on the Cuisinart and pour in the mixture.
3. Churn for 10 minutes.
4. Transfer in an airtight container and freeze overnight.

Nutrition Information:
Calories per serving:200 ; Protein: 4.5g; Carbs: 26.3g; Fat: 9.8g Sugar: 21.5g

Berry Berry Frozen Yogurt

Serves: 12
Cooking Time: 10 minutes

Ingredients:
- ¾ cup whole milk
- ¼ cup sugar
- 4 cups Greek yogurt
- 2 cups frozen mixed berries, thawed and pureed

Directions:
1. Place all ingredients in a food processor. Pulse until smooth. Place in the fridge to chill.
2. Turn on the Cuisinart and pour in the mixture.
3. Churn for 10 minutes.
4. Transfer in an airtight container and freeze overnight.

Nutrition Information:
Calories per serving: 109; Protein: 4.2g; Carbs: 14.2g; Fat: 4.2g Sugar: 13.6g

Blackberry Sugar-Free Keto Frozen Yogurt

Serves: 10
Cooking Time: 10 minutes

Ingredients:
- 4 cups blackberries
- 1 cup Greek yogurt
- 1 tablespoon lemon juice
- 1 teaspoon vanilla extract

Directions:
1. Place all ingredients in a food processor. Pulse until smooth. Place in the fridge to chill.
2. Turn on the Cuisinart and pour in the mixture.
3. Churn for 10 minutes.
4. Transfer in an airtight container and freeze overnight.

Nutrition Information:
Calories per serving: 63; Protein: 4g; Carbs: 10g; Fat: 0g Sugar: 3g

Lemon Frozen Yogurt

Serves: 4
Cooking Time: 10 minutes

Ingredients:
- ¾ cup sugar
- 2 tablespoons lemon juice
- 1/3 tablespoon lemon zest
- ½ teaspoon vanilla
- 2 cups plain yogurt

Directions:
1. Place all ingredients in a food processor. Pulse until smooth. Place in the fridge to chill.
2. Turn on the Cuisinart and pour in the mixture.
3. Churn for 10 minutes.
4. Transfer in an airtight container and freeze overnight.

Nutrition Information:
Calories per serving:151 ; Protein: 4.2g; Carbs: 25.1g; Fat: 4g Sugar: 23.4g

Lemon Blueberry Frozen Yogurt

Serves: 5
Cooking Time: 20 minutes

Ingredients:
- ½ cup fresh lemon juice
- 1 tablespoon grated lemon zest
- 2/3 cup sugar
- ¾ cup blueberries
- ¼ cup honey
- 2 cups plain whole milk yogurt
- ½ cup heavy cream

Directions:
1. In a saucepan, place the lemon juice, zest, sugar, and blueberries. Add a little water. Turn on the heat to medium low. Allow the mixture to simmer until the blueberries turn into a jam-like consistency. Set aside to cool.
2. In a cold bowl, whisk together the honey, yogurt, and heavy cream.
3. Turn on the Cuisinart and pour in the mixture.
4. Churn for 10 minutes.
5. Five minutes before the churning stops, add the blueberry mixture.
6. Transfer in an airtight container and freeze overnight.

Nutrition Information:
Calories per serving:245 ; Protein: 4.1g; Carbs: 42.6g; Fat: 7.8g Sugar: 40.5g

Maple Frozen Yogurt

Serves: 4
Cooking Time: 10 minutes

Ingredients:
- 1 cup chopped pecans
- ½ cup + 1 tablespoon maple syrup
- 2 cups non-fat Greek yogurt
- ½ cup heavy cream
- teaspoon vanilla extract
- 1 tablespoon rum

Directions:
1. Place the pecans and 1 tablespoon maple syrup in a non-stick pan and stir until the syrup becomes dry. Set aside to cool.
2. In a cold bowl, combine the yogurt, cream, maple syrup, vanilla extract, and rum.
3. Turn on the Cuisinart and pour in the mixture.
4. Churn for 10 minutes.
5. Five minutes before the churning stops, add maple pecans.
6. Transfer in an airtight container and freeze overnight.

Nutrition Information:
Calories per serving: 425; Protein: 13.9g; Carbs: 40.5g; Fat: 23.7g Sugar: 34.9g

Matcha Frozen Yogurt

Serves: 6
Cooking Time: 10 minutes

Ingredients:
- 2 cups Greek yogurt
- ¾ cup sugar
- 2 tablespoons matcha powder
- A pinch of salt

Directions:
1. In a cold bowl, combine all ingredients.
2. Turn on the Cuisinart and pour in the mixture.
3. Churn for 10 minutes.
4. Transfer in an airtight container and freeze overnight.

Nutrition Information:
Calories per serving: 106; Protein: 3.1g; Carbs: 18.1g; Fat: 2.7g Sugar: 16.2g

Peach Mango Frozen Yogurt

Serves: 5
Cooking Time: 4 minutes

Ingredients:
- 1 ½ cups Greek yogurt
- 1 cup sliced peaches
- 1 cup diced mango
- ½ cup sugar
- 1 teaspoon vanilla extract

Directions:
1. Place all ingredients in a food processor. Pulse until smooth.
2. Turn on the Cuisinart and pour in the mixture.
3. Churn for 10 minutes.
4. Transfer in an airtight container and freeze overnight.

Nutrition Information:
Calories per serving: 182; Protein: 14.8g; Carbs: 31g; Fat: 1g Sugar:29 g

Feta Frozen Yogurt

Serves: 6
Cooking Time: 10 minutes

Ingredients:
- 1 cup plain Greek yogurt
- ½ cup feta cheese
- 1 tablespoon honey

Directions:
1. Place all ingredients in a food processor. Pulse until smooth.
2. Turn on the Cuisinart and pour in the mixture.
3. Churn for 10 minutes.
4. Transfer in an airtight container and freeze overnight.

Nutrition Information:
Calories per serving: 161; Protein:7 g; Carbs: 12g; Fat: 10g Sugar: 11g

Mint Greek Frozen Yogurt

Serves: 10
Cooking Time: 10 minutes

Ingredients:
- 3 cups plain Greek yogurt
- 1 cup sugar
- ¼ cup lemon juice
- 2 teaspoons vanilla
- 1/8 teaspoon salt
- 2 tablespoons mint, chopped finely

Directions:
1. Place the yogurt, sugar, lemon juice, vanilla, and salt in a cold bowl. Whisk until smooth. Add the chopped mint.
2. Turn on the Cuisinart and pour in the mixture.
3. Churn for 10 minutes.
4. Transfer in an airtight container and freeze overnight.

Nutrition Information:
Calories per serving: 84; Protein: 2g; Carbs: 15g; Fat: 1g Sugar: 5g

Dark Chocolate Coconut Frozen Yogurt

Serves: 8
Cooking Time: 20 minutes

Ingredients:
- 1 14-ounce coconut milk
- ¼ cup honey
- 2 teaspoons cocoa powder
- 1 tablespoon arrowroot powder
- A pinch of salt
- 1 ½ cup plain yogurt
- ½ cup semi-sweet chocolate chips
- ½ cup dried coconut flakes

Directions:
1. In a saucepan, add the coconut milk, honey, cocoa, and arrowroot. Bring to a boil over low heat until the mixture slightly thickens. Make sure to mix constantly. Remove from the heat and set aside to cool.
2. In a cold bowl, mix together salt and yogurt. Add the coconut milk mixture. Whisk until smooth.
3. Turn on the Cuisinart and pour in the mixture.
4. Churn for 10 minutes.
5. Transfer in an airtight container and freeze overnight.
6. Garnish with chocolate chips and coconut flakes before serving.

Nutrition Information:
Calories per serving: 242; Protein: 4g; Carbs: 35g; Fat: 9g Sugar: 18g

Buttermilk Frozen Yogurt

Serves: 7
Cooking Time: 10 minutes

Ingredients:
- 1 cup sugar
- ½ cup light corn syrup
- ¼ cup water
- 1/8 teaspoon salt
- 2 cups whole plain Greek yogurt
- 1 cup buttermilk, shaken
- 5 teaspoons fresh lemon juice

Directions:
1. Place the sugar, corn syrup, and water in a saucepan. Bring to a boil over low heat while stirring constantly. Add the salt. Continue stirring until the sugar dissolves. Remove from heat and set aside.
2. In a cold bowl, mix together the sugar mixture, Greek yogurt, buttermilk, and lemon juice.
3. Turn on the Cuisinart and pour in the mixture.
4. Churn for 10 minutes.
5. Transfer in an airtight container and freeze overnight.
6. Garnish with chocolate chips and coconut flakes before serving.

Nutrition Information:
Calories per serving:182 ; Protein: 4g; Carbs: 38.2g; Fat: 2.6g Sugar: 37.7g

Pumpkin Frozen Yogurt

Serves: 4
Cooking Time: 10 minutes

Ingredients:
- 2 cups plain Greek yogurt
- 4 ounces low-fat cream cheese, softened
- ½ cup canned pumpkin, mashed
- ¼ cup brown sugar
- 1 tablespoon pumpkin pie spice
- 1 teaspoon vanilla extract

Directions:
1. Place all ingredients in a food processor. Pulse until smooth.
2. Turn on the Cuisinart and pour in the mixture.
3. Churn for 10 minutes.
4. Transfer in an airtight container and freeze overnight.

Nutrition Information:
Calories per serving: 198; Protein:12 g; Carbs: 24g; Fat: 7g Sugar:20 g

Watermelon Strawberry Frozen Yogurt

Serves: 12
Cooking Time: 10 minutes

Ingredients:
- 1 cup watermelon, cubed and seeds removed
- 2 cups frozen strawberries, hulled
- 1 banana, peeled
- ¼ cup honey
- A pinch of salt
- 4 cups Greek yogurt

Directions:
1. Place all ingredients in a food processor. Pulse until smooth.
2. Turn on the Cuisinart and pour in the mixture.
3. Churn for 10 minutes.
4. Transfer in an airtight container and freeze overnight.

Nutrition Information:
Calories per serving: 97; Protein: 3.2g; Carbs: 16.2g; Fat: 2.8g Sugar: 13.3g

Pistachio Berry Frozen Yogurt

Serves: 7
Cooking Time: 10 minutes

Ingredients:
- 1 cup heavy cream
- 1 cup Greek yogurt
- 1 cup milk
- ½ cup honey
- 2 tablespoons lemon juice
- ½ cup strawberries, hulled
- ¼ cup toasted pistachio nuts, chopped

Directions:
1. Place all ingredients except the pistachio nuts in a food processor. Pulse until smooth.
2. Turn on the Cuisinart and pour in the mixture.
3. Churn for 10 minutes.
4. Transfer in an airtight container and freeze overnight.
5. Garnish with pistachio nuts before serving.

Nutrition Information:
Calories per serving: 204; Protein: 3.7g; Carbs: 26g; Fat: 10.7g Sugar: 24.7g

Mulberry Frozen Yogurt

Serves: 12
Cooking Time: 10 minutes

Ingredients:
- 2 cups heavy cream
- 1 ½ cups Greek yogurt
- 1 cup milk
- ½ cup honey
- 2 tablespoons lemon juice
- ½ cup mulberries

Directions:
1. Place all ingredients in a food processor. Pulse until smooth.
2. Turn on the Cuisinart and pour in the mixture.
3. Churn for 10 minutes.
4. Transfer in an airtight container and freeze overnight.
5. Garnish with pistachio nuts before serving.

Nutrition Information:
Calories per serving: 157; Protein: 6.3g; Carbs: 15.7g; Fat: 8.3g Sugar: 15.3g

Sorbets

Mango Tango Sorbet

Serves: 5
Cooking Time: 10 minutes

Ingredients:
- 2 ripe mangoes, peeled and diced
- 1 cup white sugar
- 1 lime, juiced
- 2 cups tangerine juice

Directions:
1. Place all ingredients in a blender. Pulse until smooth.
2. Turn on the Cuisinart and pour in the mixture.
3. Churn for 10 minutes.
4. Transfer in an airtight container and freeze overnight.

Nutrition Information:
Calories per serving: 256; Protein: 1.2g; Carbs: 66g; Fat: 0g Sugar:55 g

Meyer Lemon Sorbet

Serves: 3
Cooking Time: 15 minutes

Ingredients:
- 1 cup water
- 1 cup sugar
- 2 teaspoons lemon zest
- 1 cup lemon juice, freshly squeezed

Directions:
1. Place all ingredients in a saucepan. Turn on the heat and allow to simmer for 5 minutes or until the sugar dissolves.
2. Remove from the heat and place in the fridge to cool for 2 hours.
3. Turn on the Cuisinart and pour in the mixture.
4. Churn for 10 minutes.
5. Transfer in an airtight container and freeze overnight.

Nutrition Information:
Calories per serving:148 ; Protein: 0.3g; Carbs: 39.1g; Fat: 0.2g Sugar: 34.7g

Orange Sorbet

Serves: 7
Cooking Time: 15 minutes

Ingredients:
- 1 orange, zest, and juice
- 2 cups water
- 1 1/3 cups sugar
- 3 cups fresh orange juice
- 4 tablespoons lemon juice

Directions:
1. Place all ingredients in a saucepan. Turn on the heat and allow to simmer for 5 minutes or until the sugar dissolves.
2. Remove from the heat and place in the fridge to cool for 2 hours.
3. Turn on the Cuisinart and pour in the mixture.
4. Churn for 10 minutes.
5. Transfer in an airtight container and freeze overnight.

Nutrition Information:
Calories per serving: 146; Protein: 1g; Carbs: 35.9g; Fat: 0.2g Sugar: 30.6g

Lemon Strawberry Sorbet

Serves: 6
Cooking Time: 15 minutes

Ingredients:
- 1 cup water
- 1 cup sugar
- 2 teaspoons lemon zest
- 1 cup lemon juice, freshly squeezed
- 1 cup fresh strawberries, hulled

Directions:
1. Place the water and sugar in a saucepan and bring to a boil over medium heat until the sugar dissolves. Remove from the heat and place in the fridge to chill for at least 3 hours.
2. Once cooled, place the water-sugar mixture into a blender and add the rest of the ingredients. Pulse until smooth.
3. Turn on the Cuisinart and pour in the mixture.
4. Churn for 10 minutes.
5. Transfer in an airtight container and freeze overnight.

Nutrition Information:
Calories per serving: 82; Protein: 0.3g; Carbs: 21.4g; Fat: 0.2g Sugar: 18.5g

Watermelon Sorbet

Serves: 7
Cooking Time: 15 minutes

Ingredients:
- 1 cup sugar
- 1 cup water
- ¼ cup lemon juice
- 3 cups watermelon, peeled and seeded

Directions:
1. Place the water and sugar in a saucepan and bring to a boil over medium heat until the sugar dissolves. Remove from the heat and place in the fridge to chill for at least 3 hours.
2. Once cooled, place the water-sugar mixture into a blender and add the rest of the ingredients. Pulse until smooth.
3. Turn on the Cuisinart and pour in the mixture.
4. Churn for 10 minutes.
5. Transfer in an airtight container and freeze overnight.

Nutrition Information:
Calories per serving: 77; Protein: 0.4g; Carbs: 19.8g; Fat: 0.1g Sugar: 12.3g

Easy Coconut Sorbet

Serves: 6
Cooking Time: 15 minutes

Ingredients:
- 1 cup coconut water
- ¾ cup sugar
- 2 cans coconut milk

Directions:
1. Place coconut water and sugar in a saucepan. Bring to a boil until the sugar dissolves.
2. Remove from the heat and place in the fridge to chill for at least 3 hours.
3. Turn on the Cuisinart and pour in the water-sugar mixture and coconut milk.
4. Churn for 10 minutes.
5. Transfer in an airtight container and freeze overnight.

Nutrition Information:
Calories per serving: 69; Protein: 0.8g; Carbs: 16.5g; Fat: 0.2g Sugar: 15.1g

Mango Pineapple Sorbet

Serves: 6
Cooking Time: 10 minutes

Ingredients:
- 1 cup fresh ripe mango, peeled and cubed (seed removed)
- 1 cup pineapple tidbits
- ¼ cup water
- 1 teaspoon lemon juice
- ½ cup sugar
- ½ teaspoon salt

Directions:
1. Place all ingredients in a blender. Pulse until smooth.
2. Place in the fridge to chill for 2 hours.
3. Turn on the Cuisinart and pour in the mixture.
4. Churn for 10 minutes.
5. Transfer in an airtight container and freeze overnight

Nutrition Information:
Calories per serving:74 ; Protein: 0.4g; Carbs: 19g; Fat: 0.1g Sugar: 10g

Lime Sorbet

Serves: 7
Cooking Time: 15 minutes

Ingredients:
- 2 cups water
- 1 cup sugar
- 4 limes, zest
- Juice from 8 limes

Directions:
1. Place the water and sugar in a saucepan. Bring to a boil until the sugar dissolves.
2. Remove from the heat and place in the fridge to chill for at least 3 hours.
3. Turn on the Cuisinart and pour in the water-sugar mixture, lime zest, and lime juice.
4. Churn for 10 minutes.
5. Transfer in an airtight container and freeze overnight.

Nutrition Information:
Calories per serving:74 ; Protein: 0.3g; Carbs: 20.6g; Fat: 0.1g Sugar: 13 g

Strawberry, Nectarine, Orange, Banana Sorbet

Serves: 8
Cooking Time: 10 minutes

Ingredients:
- ¾ cup sugar
- ¾ cup water
- 1 cup strawberries, hulled
- 1 cup orange wedges, peeled and seeds removed
- 1 cup nectarine, peeled and seeds removed
- 1 ripe banana, peeled

Directions:
1. Place the water and sugar in a saucepan. Bring to a boil until the sugar dissolves.
2. Remove from the heat and place in the fridge to chill for at least 3 hours.
3. Place the rest of the ingredients in a blender and add the chilled sugar mixture. Pulse until smooth. Allow to chill for another two hours.
4. Turn on the Cuisinart and pour in the mixture.
5. Churn for 10 minutes.
6. Transfer in an airtight container and freeze overnight.

Nutrition Information:
Calories per serving: 78; Protein: 0.7g; Carbs: 20g; Fat: 0g Sugar: 14g

Kiwi Sorbet

Serves: 6
Cooking Time: 15 minutes

Ingredients:
- ¾ cup granulated sugar
- ¾ cup water
- 2 pounds ripe kiwi fruit, peeled and sliced

Directions:
1. Place the water and sugar in a saucepan. Bring to a boil until the sugar dissolves.
2. Remove from the heat and place in the fridge to chill for at least 3 hours.
3. Place the kiwi slices in a blender and add the chilled sugar mixture. Pulse until smooth. Allow to chill for another two hours.
4. Turn on the Cuisinart and pour in the mixture.
5. Churn for 10 minutes.
6. Transfer in an airtight container and freeze overnight.

Nutrition Information:
Calories per serving: 159; Protein: 0.6g; Carbs: 41.1g; Fat: 0.1g Sugar: 39.3g

Pineapple Sorbet

Serves: 5
Cooking Time: 10 minutes

Ingredients:
- 1 small pineapple, peeled and cored
- 2 tablespoons fresh lemon juice
- 1 cup sugar

Directions:
1. Place all ingredients in a blender. Pulse until smooth.
2. Place in the fridge to chill for at least 2 hours.
3. Turn on the Cuisinart and pour in the mixture.
4. Churn for 10 minutes.
5. Transfer in an airtight container and freeze overnight.

Nutrition Information:
Calories per serving: 170; Protein: 1g; Carbs: 44g; Fat: 0.2g Sugar: 25g

Avocado Sorbet

Serves: 5
Cooking Time: 20 minutes

Ingredients:
- 2/3 to ¾ cup avocado meat, cut into chunks
- ½ cup agave syrup
- ½ cup coconut milk
- ¼ cup fresh lime juice

Directions:
1. Place all ingredients in a blender and pulse until smooth.
2. Turn on the Cuisinart and pour in the mixture.
3. Churn for 10 minutes.
4. Transfer in an airtight container and freeze overnight.

Nutrition Information:
Calories per serving: 159; Protein: 1.1g; Carbs: 21g; Fat: 8.8g Sugar: 11g

Peach Sorbet

Serves: 8
Cooking Time: 15 minutes

Ingredients:
- 2/3 cup sugar
- 1 cup water
- 2 ½ pounds peaches, peeled and halved (seeds removed)
- 3 tablespoons fresh lemon juice
- ½ teaspoon lemon zest

Directions:
1. Place sugar and water in a saucepan. Bring to a boil until the sugar dissolves. Add the peaches and simmer for another 3 minutes.
2. Remove from the heat and place in the fridge to chill for at least 3 hours.
3. Place all ingredients in a blender and add the chilled sugar mixture. Pulse until smooth. Allow to chill for another two hours.
4. Turn on the Cuisinart and pour in the mixture.
5. Churn for 10 minutes.
6. Transfer in an airtight container and freeze overnight.

Nutrition Information:
Calories per serving: 121; Protein: 1g; Carbs: 31g; Fat: 0g Sugar: 25g

Lime-Mango Sorbet

Serves: 8
Cooking Time: 15 minutes

Ingredients:
- ½ cup water
- ¼ cup sugar
- 5 cups ripe mango cubes
- 1 teaspoon lime zest
- ¼ lime juice

Directions:
1. Place sugar and water in a saucepan. Bring to a boil until the sugar dissolves.
2. Remove from the heat and place in the fridge to chill for at least 3 hours.
3. Place all ingredients in a blender and add the chilled sugar mixture. Pulse until smooth. Allow to chill for another two hours.
4. Turn on the Cuisinart and pour in the mixture.
5. Churn for 10 minutes.
6. Transfer in an airtight container and freeze overnight.

Nutrition Information:
Calories per serving: 88; Protein: 1g; Carbs: 22g; Fat: 1g Sugar: 19g

Summer Sorbet

Serves: 6
Cooking Time: 15 minutes

Ingredients:
- 2 pounds fresh fruit of your choice
- 8 ounces sugar
- ¼ cup lemon juice
- ¼ cup vodka

Directions:
1. Place all ingredients in a blender. Pulse until smooth.
2. Place in the fridge and allow to chill for at least 3 hours.
3. Turn on the Cuisinart and pour in the mixture.
4. Churn for 10 minutes.
5. Transfer in an airtight container and freeze overnight.

Nutrition Information:
Calories per serving: 268; Protein: 0.8g; Carbs: 67.4g; Fat: 0.8g Sugar: 54.6g

Berries Sorbet

Serves: 8
Cooking Time: 15 minutes

Ingredients:
- 1/3 cup water
- ¼ cup sugar
- 1 12-ounce package frozen blackberries
- 4 cups mixed berries

Directions:
1. Place water and sugar in a saucepan. Bring to a boil until sugar dissolves. Remove from heat and allow to chill in the fridge for at least 2 hours.
2. Place all ingredients in a blender. Pulse until smooth.
3. Turn on the Cuisinart and pour in the mixture.
4. Churn for 10 minutes.
5. Transfer in an airtight container and freeze overnight.

Nutrition Information:
Calories per serving:299 ; Protein: 4.3g; Carbs: 56.5g; Fat: 7.2g Sugar: 20.1g

Passion Fruit Sorbet

Serves: 8
Cooking Time: 15 minutes

Ingredients:
- 1 cup boiling water
- ¾ cup sugar
- 8 passion fruit, flesh scooped
- Juice from 1 lemon

Directions:
1. Place water and sugar in a saucepan. Bring to a boil until sugar dissolves. Remove from heat and allow to chill in the fridge for at least 2 hours.
2. While the sugar syrup is chilling, place the passion fruit in a blender and pulse until smooth. Pass the mixture into a sieve to remove the seeds. Discard the seeds and save the juice.
3. Mix the passion fruit juice with the sugar syrup and add the lemon juice.
4. Turn on the Cuisinart and pour in the mixture.
5. Churn for 10 minutes.
6. Transfer in an airtight container and freeze overnight.

Nutrition Information:
Calories per serving:55 ; Protein: 0.4g; Carbs: 13.9g; Fat: 0.2g Sugar: 6g

Grape Sorbet

Serves: 6
Cooking Time: 10 minutes

Ingredients:
- 4 cups seedless grapes
- 1/3 cup granulated sugar
- 2 tablespoon lemon juice

Directions:
1. Place the grapes and sugar in a blender and pulse until smooth.
2. Pass the mixture through a sieve to remove the skin.
3. Add the lemon juice to the grape puree.
4. Turn on the Cuisinart and pour in the mixture.
5. Churn for 10 minutes.
6. Transfer in an airtight container and freeze overnight.

Nutrition Information:
Calories per serving: 100; Protein: 1g; Carbs: 26g; Fat: 0g Sugar: 18g

Cherry Mango Sorbet

Serves: 2
Cooking Time: 15 minutes

Ingredients:
- 1 cup frozen mango chunks
- ½ cup frozen pineapple chunks
- 1 cup preserved cherries
- 1 tablespoon water

Directions:
1. Place all ingredients in a blender. Pulse until smooth.
2. Turn on the Cuisinart and pour in the mixture.
3. Churn for 15 minutes.
4. Transfer in an airtight container and freeze overnight.

Nutrition Information:
Calories per serving:202 ; Protein: 1.7g; Carbs: 51.7g; Fat: 0.3g Sugar: 32g

Mulberry Ginger Sorbet

Serves: 8
Cooking Time: 20 minutes

Ingredients:
- ¾ cup sugar
- ¾ cup water
- Juice from 1 tablespoon grated ginger
- 4 cups mulberries
- 2 tablespoon raspberry liqueur

Directions:
1. Place water and sugar in a saucepan. Bring to a boil until sugar dissolves. Remove from heat and allow to chill in the fridge for at least 2 hours.
2. Place all ingredients in a blender and pulse until smooth.
3. Turn on the Cuisinart and pour in the mixture.
4. Churn for 15 minutes.
5. Transfer in an airtight container and freeze overnight.

Nutrition Information:
Calories per serving: 71; Protein: 1.1g; Carbs: 17.4g; Fat: 0.3g Sugar: 8g

Frozen Ice Cream Desserts

Frozen Banana Split

Serves: 15
Cooking Time: 25 minutes

Ingredients:
- 1 cup cold whole milk
- ¾ cup granulated sugar
- 2 cups cold heavy cream
- 1 teaspoon vanilla extract
- 4 bananas, split lengthwise
- 16 ounces whipped cream
- 1 cup salted peanuts
- 1 cup chocolate syrup

Directions:
1. Put ice water in a large mixing bowl. Place a small bowl on top of the large bowl with ice. Pour cold milk and sugar into the small bowl and whisk until the sugar is dissolved. Stir in the cream and vanilla. Stir to combine.
2. Place the cold freezer bowl in the Cuisinart Ice Cream Maker. Turn on the machine and pour in the mixture. Stop in 25 minutes until the mixture becomes soft and creamy.
3. Transfer into an air-tight container and freeze overnight.
4. Once the ice cream is frozen, assemble the banana split.
5. Place two slices of the banana on each side of a serving dish and place three scoops of ice cream in between.
6. Top with whipped cream and garnish with peanuts.
7. Drizzle with chocolate syrup on top.

Nutrition Information:
Calories per serving:334 ; Protein: 6.5g; Carbs: 32.6g; Fat: 21.2g Sugar: 19.5g

Turtle Brownie Ice Cream

Serves: 8
Cooking Time: 25 minutes

Ingredients:
- 1 cup cold whole milk
- ¾ cup granulated sugar
- 2 cups cold heavy cream
- 1 teaspoon vanilla extract
- 1 package commercial brownie

Directions:
1. Put ice water in a large mixing bowl. Place a small bowl on top of the large bowl with ice. Pour cold milk and sugar into the small bowl and whisk until the sugar is dissolved. Stir in the cream and vanilla. Stir to combine.
2. Place the cold freezer bowl in the Cuisinart Ice Cream Maker. Turn on the machine and pour in the mixture. Stop in 25 minutes until the mixture becomes soft and creamy.
3. Transfer into an air-tight container and freeze overnight.
4. Once the ice cream is frozen, assemble the frozen brownie.
5. Slice the brownies into 2x2 inch squares.
6. Spread the vanilla ice cream in between two brownie slices.
7. Serve immediately.

Nutrition Information:
Calories per serving: 200; Protein: 1.9g; Carbs: 19.1g; Fat: 13.3g Sugar: 17g

Oreo Ice Cream Cake

Serves: 16
Cooking Time: 25 minutes

Ingredients:
- 1 cup cold whole milk
- ¾ cup granulated sugar
- 2 cups cold heavy cream
- 1 teaspoon vanilla extract
- 2 small packages Oreos, crushed
- ¼ cup butter
- 8-ounce whipped cream
- 16-ounce hot fudge

Directions:
1. Put ice water in a large mixing bowl. Place a small bowl on top of the large bowl with ice. Pour cold milk and sugar into the small bowl and whisk until the sugar is dissolved. Stir in the cream and vanilla. Stir to combine.
2. Place the cold freezer bowl in the Cuisinart Ice Cream Maker. Turn on the machine and pour in the mixture. Add one package of crushed Oreos five minutes before the time ends.
3. Stop in 25 minutes until the mixture becomes soft and creamy.
4. In a bowl, mix the remaining crushed Oreos and butter to create a dough.
5. Press the Oreo dough in a spring form pan.
6. Spread the ice cream over the crust and freeze for 4 hours in the fridge.
7. Before serving, top with whipped cream and drizzle with hot fudge.

Nutrition Information:
Calories per serving: 689; Protein: 10g; Carbs: 82g; Fat:35 g Sugar: 67g

Strawberry Ice Cream Milk Shake

Serves: 8
Cooking Time: 30 minutes

Ingredients:
- 1 cup cold whole milk
- ¾ cup granulated sugar
- 2 cups cold heavy cream
- 1 teaspoon vanilla extract
- 1 cup strawberries hulled
- ½ cup ice

Directions:
1. Put ice water in a large mixing bowl. Place a small bowl on top of the large bowl with ice. Pour cold milk and sugar into the small bowl and whisk until the sugar is dissolved. Stir in the cream and vanilla. Stir to combine.
2. Place the cold freezer bowl in the Cuisinart Ice Cream Maker. Turn on the machine and pour in the mixture. Add one package of crushed Oreos five minutes before the time ends.
3. Stop in 25 minutes until the mixture becomes soft and creamy.
4. Transfer into an air-tight container and freeze overnight.
5. Place strawberries, ice, and 2 cups of milkshake in a blender. Pulse until smooth.
6. Serve immediately.

Nutrition Information:
Calories per serving:193 ; Protein: 1.9g; Carbs: 17.4g; Fat: 13.1g Sugar: 7g

Vanilla Ice Cream Sponge Cake

Serves: 12
Cooking Time: 25 minutes

Ingredients:
- 1 cup cold whole milk
- ¾ cup granulated sugar
- 2 cups cold heavy cream
- 1 teaspoon vanilla extract
- 1-pound sponge cake, sliced to 1-inch thick
- 1 cup strawberry slices
- Whipped cream

Directions:
1. Put ice water in a large mixing bowl. Place a small bowl on top of the large bowl with ice. Pour cold milk and sugar into the small bowl and whisk until the sugar is dissolved. Stir in the cream and vanilla. Stir to combine.
2. Place the cold freezer bowl in the Cuisinart Ice Cream Maker. Turn on the machine and pour in the mixture. Add one package of crushed Oreos five minutes before the time ends.
3. Stop in 25 minutes until the mixture becomes soft and creamy.
4. Transfer into an air-tight container and freeze overnight.
5. In a springform pan, place slices of sponge cake.
6. Spread ice cream on top and top with strawberry slices.
7. Repeat the process until you make three layers of sponge cake, ice cream, and strawberry.
8. Top with whipped cream.
9. Place in the fridge to set for two hours.

Nutrition Information:
Calories per serving:281 ; Protein: 3.9g; Carbs: 38.3g; Fat: 12.7g Sugar: 20.3g

Vanilla Peanut Butter Layer

Serves: 5
Cooking Time: 25 minutes

Ingredients:
- 1 cup cold whole milk
- ¾ cup granulated sugar
- 2 cups cold heavy cream
- 1 teaspoon vanilla extract
- 2 packs graham cracker, crushed
- ½ cup smooth peanut butter
- ¼ cup toasted peanuts, crushed

Directions:
1. Put ice water in a large mixing bowl. Place a small bowl on top of the large bowl with ice. Pour cold milk and sugar into the small bowl and whisk until the sugar is dissolved. Stir in the cream and vanilla. Stir to combine.
2. Place the cold freezer bowl in the Cuisinart Ice Cream Maker. Turn on the machine and pour in the mixture. Add one package of crushed Oreos five minutes before the time ends.
3. Stop in 25 minutes until the mixture becomes soft and creamy.
4. Transfer into an air-tight container and freeze overnight.
5. Assemble the dessert by putting crushed graham cracker in the bottom of a parfait glass then layer with vanilla ice cream and peanut butter.
6. Repeat until three layers are formed.
7. Garnish with toasted peanuts.
8. Serve immediately.

Nutrition Information:
Calories per serving: 521; Protein: 14.1g; Carbs: 42.8g; Fat: 34.5g Sugar:24.9 g

Oreo Ice Cream Bar Dessert

Serves: 8
Cooking Time: 25 minutes

Ingredients:
- 1 cup cold whole milk
- ¾ cup granulated sugar
- 2 cups cold heavy cream
- 1 teaspoon vanilla extract
- 36 pieces Oreo cookies, crushed
- 6 tablespoons melted butter
- 1 cup commercial chocolate syrup
- 1 cup whipping cream

Directions:
1. Put ice water in a large mixing bowl. Place a small bowl on top of the large bowl with ice. Pour cold milk and sugar into the small bowl and whisk until the sugar is dissolved. Stir in the cream and vanilla. Stir to combine.
2. Place the cold freezer bowl in the Cuisinart Ice Cream Maker. Turn on the machine and pour in the mixture. Add one package of crushed Oreos five minutes before the time ends.
3. Stop in 25 minutes until the mixture becomes soft and creamy.
4. Transfer into an air-tight container and freeze overnight.
5. Prepare the cookie dough by mixing together crushed Oreo cookies, melted butter, and chocolate syrup. Mix until a dough is formed.
6. Use half of the dough mixture and press firmly into a baking pan. Spread ice cream evenly on top. Place in the fridge and allow cream to freeze.
7. Once frozen, press the remaining dough on top.
8. Serve with whipped cream.

Nutrition Information:
Calories per serving: 512; Protein: 8g; Carbs: 56g; Fat:30 g Sugar:43 g

Caramel Frozen Squares

Serves: 8
Cooking Time: 25 minutes

Ingredients:
- 1 cup cold whole milk
- ¾ cup granulated sugar
- 2 cups cold heavy cream
- 1 teaspoon vanilla extract
- 1 ½ cups packed light brown sugar
- ½ cup evaporated milk
- 7 tablespoons butter, melted
- ½ teaspoon vanilla extract
- 1 13-ounce packaged pecan shortbread cookies, crushed

Directions:
1. Put ice water in a large mixing bowl. Place a small bowl on top of the large bowl with ice. Pour cold milk and sugar into the small bowl and whisk until the sugar is dissolved. Stir in the cream and vanilla. Stir to combine.
2. Place the cold freezer bowl in the Cuisinart Ice Cream Maker. Turn on the machine and pour in the mixture. Add one package of crushed Oreos five minutes before the time ends.
3. Stop in 25 minutes until the mixture becomes soft and creamy.
4. Transfer into an air-tight container and freeze overnight.
5. In a saucepan over medium flame, mix together the brown sugar and milk. Bring to a boil and allow to simmer for 3 minutes. Remove from heat add a tablespoon of butter and vanilla. Set aside. This will be the caramel sauce.
6. Coat a 9x13 inch pan with cooking spray and press the crumb into the dish.
7. Spread the ice cream carefully and evenly on top. Top with the remaining cookie crumbs and pour in sauce.

Nutrition Information:
Calories per serving:539 ; Protein: 4.9g; Carbs: 44.7g; Fat: 38.4g Sugar: 16g

Frozen Pistachio Ice Cream Dessert

Serves: 6
Cooking Time: 30 minutes

Ingredients:
- 1 cup cold whole milk
- ¾ cup granulated sugar
- 2 cups cold heavy cream
- 1 teaspoon vanilla extract
- 45 pieces Ritz crackers, crushed
- ¾ cup melted butter
- 2 small pistachio pudding mix
- Chocolate chips

Directions:
1. Put ice water in a large mixing bowl. Place a small bowl on top of the large bowl with ice. Pour cold milk and sugar into the small bowl and whisk until the sugar is dissolved. Stir in the cream and vanilla. Stir to combine.
2. Place the cold freezer bowl in the Cuisinart Ice Cream Maker. Turn on the machine and pour in the mixture. Add one package of crushed Oreos five minutes before the time ends.
3. Stop in 25 minutes until the mixture becomes soft and creamy.
4. Transfer into an air-tight container and freeze overnight.
5. In a bowl, combine the crackers and butter. Mix until combined.
6. Press dough in individual bowls or ramekins. Set aside.
7. Place ice cream in another bowl and add the pudding mix.
8. Scoop into prepared bowls and top with chocolate chips.

Nutrition Information:
Calories per serving: 563; Protein: 4.8g; Carbs: 41.9g; Fat: 42.5g Sugar: 24.6g

Ice Cream Sliders

Serves: 6
Cooking Time: 25 minutes

Ingredients:
- 1 cup cold whole milk
- ¾ cup granulated sugar
- 2 cups cold heavy cream
- 1 teaspoon vanilla extract
- 10 pieces vanilla wafers
- Toppings of your choice (nuts, graham crackers, marshmallows)
- Commercial caramel sauce

Directions:
1. Put ice water in a large mixing bowl. Place a small bowl on top of the large bowl with ice. Pour cold milk and sugar into the small bowl and whisk until the sugar is dissolved. Stir in the cream and vanilla. Stir to combine.
2. Place the cold freezer bowl in the Cuisinart Ice Cream Maker. Turn on the machine and pour in the mixture. Add one package of crushed Oreos five minutes before the time ends.
3. Stop in 25 minutes until the mixture becomes soft and creamy.
4. Transfer into an air-tight container and freeze overnight.
5. Place the ice cream on a bowl and top with wafers and toppings of your choice. Drizzle with caramel sauce.
6. Serve immediately.

Nutrition Information:
Calories per serving: 352; Protein: 3.1g; Carbs: 44.1g; Fat: 18.5g Sugar: 31.6g

Sugar Cookie Sandwich with Ice Cream

Serves: 10
Cooking Time: 25 minutes

Ingredients:
- 1 cup cold whole milk
- ¾ cup granulated sugar
- 2 cups cold heavy cream
- 1 teaspoon vanilla extract
- 20 cinnamon sugar cookies

Directions:
1. Put ice water in a large mixing bowl. Place a small bowl on top of the large bowl with ice. Pour cold milk and sugar into the small bowl and whisk until the sugar is dissolved. Stir in the cream and vanilla. Stir to combine.
2. Place the cold freezer bowl in the Cuisinart Ice Cream Maker. Turn on the machine and pour in the mixture. Add one package of crushed Oreos five minutes before the time ends.
3. Stop in 25 minutes until the mixture becomes soft and creamy.
4. Transfer into an air-tight container and freeze overnight.
5. Spread the ice cream in between two sugar cookies.
6. Serve immediately.

Nutrition Information:
Calories per serving:369 ; Protein: 6g; Carbs: 54g; Fat: 14.6g Sugar: 37.1g

Ice Cream Pizza

Serves: 8
Cooking Time: 30 minutes

Ingredients:
- 1 cup cold whole milk
- ¾ cup granulated sugar
- 2 cups cold heavy cream
- 1 teaspoon vanilla extract
- 1 commercial pizza dough, cooked according to package instructions
- 5 pieces Oreo cookies, crushed
- ½ cups M&Ms, chopped
- ½ cup hot fudge sauce

Directions:
1. Put ice water in a large mixing bowl. Place a small bowl on top of the large bowl with ice. Pour cold milk and sugar into the small bowl and whisk until the sugar is dissolved. Stir in the cream and vanilla. Stir to combine.
2. Place the cold freezer bowl in the Cuisinart Ice Cream Maker. Turn on the machine and pour in the mixture. Add one package of crushed Oreos five minutes before the time ends.
3. Stop in 25 minutes until the mixture becomes soft and creamy.
4. Transfer into an air-tight container and freeze overnight.
5. Spread ice cream in a dough and top with Oreo cookies and M&Ms. Drizzle with hot fudge sauce.
6. Slice and serve.

Nutrition Information:
Calories per serving:387 ; Protein: 11g; Carbs: 35.9g; Fat: 22.7g Sugar: 19.8g

Berry Ice Cream Cake

Serves: 8
Cooking Time:25 minutes

Ingredients:
- 1 cup graham crackers, crushed
- ¼ cup butter
- 1 cup cold whole milk
- ¾ cup granulated sugar
- 2 cups cold heavy cream
- 1 teaspoon vanilla extract
- 2 cups of frozen berries, assorted

Directions:
1. In a bowl, mix together the graham crackers and butter to form a dough. Press dough in spring form pan and place in the fridge to chill.
2. Put ice water in a large mixing bowl. Place a small bowl on top of the large bowl with ice. Pour cold milk and sugar into the small bowl and whisk until the sugar is dissolved. Stir in the cream and vanilla. Stir to combine.
3. Place the cold freezer bowl in the Cuisinart Ice Cream Maker. Turn on the machine and pour in the mixture. Add one package of crushed Oreos five minutes before the time ends.
4. Stop in 25 minutes until the mixture becomes soft and creamy.
5. Transfer into a prepared spring form pan and top with berries of your choice.
6. Freeze for 4 hours.
7. Cut into wedges before serving.

Nutrition Information:
Calories per serving:277 ; Protein: 2.9g; Carbs: 23.8g; Fat: 19.5g Sugar: 23g

Rhubarb Ice Cream Cake

Serves: 16
Cooking Time: 35 minutes

Ingredients:
- 4 stalks fresh rhubarb, chopped
- 1 medium gala apple, chopped
- ½ cup water
- 1 cup raspberries
- ½ cup white sugar
- 1 cup cold whole milk
- ¾ cup granulated sugar
- 2 cups cold heavy cream
- 1 teaspoon vanilla extract

Directions:
1. Place in a bowl the rhubarb, apple, water, raspberries, and sugar. Boil over medium flame and simmer for 10 minutes. Drain and set aside in the fridge. Reserve the juices.
2. In a bowl, mix together the graham crackers and butter to form a dough. Press dough in spring form pan and place in the fridge to chill.
3. Put ice water in a large mixing bowl. Place a small bowl on top of the large bowl with ice. Pour cold milk and sugar into the small bowl and whisk until the sugar is dissolved. Stir in the cream and vanilla. Stir to combine.
4. Place the cold freezer bowl in the Cuisinart Ice Cream Maker. Turn on the machine and pour in the mixture. Add one package of crushed Oreos five minutes before the time ends.
5. Stop in 25 minutes until the mixture becomes soft and creamy.
6. Place in a spring form pan and top with the chilled fruit sauce.

Nutrition Information:
Calories per serving: 121; Protein:1.22 g; Carbs: 13.8g; Fat: 7.3g Sugar: 12.2g

Frozen Nanaimo Pie

Serves: 16
Cooking Time: 40 minutes

Ingredients:
- ¾ cup graham cracker crumbs
- 1/3 cup shredded coconut
- 1/3 cup chopped walnut
- ¼ cup cocoa powder
- ¼ cup brown sugar
- 1/3 cup melted butter
- 1 cup cold whole milk
- ¾ cup granulated sugar
- 2 cups cold heavy cream
- 1 teaspoon vanilla extract
- 2 tablespoons semi-sweet chocolate, chopped
- ¼ cup whipping cream

Directions:
1. In a bowl, combine the graham crackers, coconut, walnut, cocoa powder, brown sugar, and butter to form a dough.
2. Press the dough in a spring form pan and set aside in the fridge to set.
3. In a bowl, mix together the graham crackers and butter to form a dough. Press dough in spring form pan and place in the fridge to chill.
4. Put ice water in a large mixing bowl. Place a small bowl on top of the large bowl with ice. Pour cold milk and sugar into the small bowl and whisk until the sugar is dissolved. Stir in the cream and vanilla. Stir to combine.
5. Place the cold freezer bowl in the Cuisinart Ice Cream Maker. Turn on the machine and pour in the mixture. Add one package of crushed Oreos five minutes before the time ends.
6. Stop in 25 minutes until the mixture becomes soft and creamy.
7. Pour into the prepared pan and top with whipping cream and chocolate chips.

Nutrition Information:
Calories per serving: 151; Protein: 1.4g; Carbs: 12.3g; Fat: 11.36g Sugar: 5.3g

CPSIA information can be obtained
at www.ICGtesting.com
Printed in the USA
LVHW100710280321
682460LV00008B/48

9 781649 841575